Damaged Spirits

Jennifer Lively

First published by Dog Ear Publishing
4010 W. 86th Street, Ste H
Indianapolis, IN 46268
www.dogearpublishing.net

ISBN: 978-1-4575-2289-5

This book is printed on acid-free paper.

Printed in the United States of America

Disclaimer

One of my favorite writers, Martha Gelhorn stated "cast your characters as fiction because the way you make the facts come alive is by showing there effects on people through stories and characters that are so closely modeled on real people that for all purposes are real."

The purpose of these vignettes is to make the reader aware of addiction as a real and recoverable condition if recognized and treated appropriately. It is my intention to create characters that you will feel a connection, and hopefully be able to relate to. Yet, as real as I want these characters to appear be aware that any similarity to anyone living or deceased in any of these stories is completely coincidental – All situations are real and the characters are genuine but the stories are completely fictional.

Preface

Addiction is a disease of excess. This disease can affect anyone at any time. No one is guaranteed immunity. Yet, unlike any other disease addictions continue to be stigmatized, scrutinized and judged by society. Visions of stereotypical toothless, bone-thin addicts and drunks living in squalor reeking of their own urine are often the first thoughts that come to mind when someone is labeled an addict. We, as a society have created "skid-row "and "crack-ally" as the geographical whereabouts of the elusive and alien addicts. We "prefer" to believe that addicts look, act and live a specific way so we can safely separate our-selves from them. We have relegated them to the darkest, fur-thermost limits of our imaginations. The reality is anyone, anywhere may be an addict. The well dressed businessman, the articulate professional, the savvy soccer coach, the scholarly pro-fessor and the charming grocery clerk can just as easily be an addict. Addicts come in all shapes, sizes, and ethnic origins. Addiction does not discriminate, the wealthy and the poor, young and old ; no one is immune.

The reaction of family and friends to a diagnosis of a loved one being an addict brings mixed reactions. They are often mortified at the prospect of a loved one being an addict and ini-tially feel embarrassed, humiliated and dishonored. Emotions run the course of denial, blame and justification. People tend to look more favorably on a mental health diagnosis than one of addiction because of the negative stigma attached to addic-tion.. The image of the stereotypical addict further alienates and complicates the possibility of treatment and ultimately the addict's recovery.

This book is for the addict who has yet to admit their problem or someone who has admitted a problem but feels alone and unique.

This book is for the family members who want to better understand and be aware of the mindset of the addict.

This book is for professionals in related fields such as medical, mental, and public health sectors. People working with criminal justice and legal clients; the educational realm as well as scholarly domains can benefit from these profiles, and those whom inadvertently work with addicts. Only after addiction rears its head in our home, our community and our schools, and is addressed appropriately, will the myth of the stereotypical addict be defeated.

May these stories enhance your understanding and intellectual perception of all addicts.

Our eccentricities set us apart from the crowd. It is our eclectic nature; our idiosyncrasies that make us unique, sometimes brilliant, often tragic. Although similar, it's not how we are alike but rather how we are different that we have a common bond. We are prone to excess - we understand the concept of balance but we defy it. We are addicts.

—Jennifer Lively

Dedication

To the independent thinkers and fearless activists
who carved a path through life's mediocrity
making it possible for me to do the work I love
and write this book.

Dorothea Dix, Mother Jones, Martha Gelhorn,
Geraldine Delaney, Arlene Savakas

Table of Contents

"Pride is the mother of arrogance."

—Toba Beta

Mrs. Michaels' Companion

The pretty young brunette hostess seemed to cringe as the pair entered the cafe. Her welcoming smile changed to fearful recognition. Mrs. Michaels was a regular, someone no one wanted as a customer. Servers consistently requested not to be her server - in fact many avoided her completely. Mrs. Michaels tipped well but money wasn't the issue. She just wasn't nice. Never. Often she dined alone but today she had a companion with her. Mrs. Michaels' companion was a younger women; younger than Mrs. Michaels but older than the hostess. The hostess prepared herself to approach the duo by first pausing then taking a deep breath. Her voice took on a high pitched tone laced with false confidence.

"Good afternoon Mrs. Michaels, you are looking well, will that be a table for two?"

Looking past the anxious hostess Mrs. Michaels abruptly responded "Yes Sweetie, I'd like that booth near the window".

Mrs. Michaels wore the cloak of condescension majestically as she slowly and purposely strode behind the nervous hostess, her hesitant companion following behind.

"no sweetie, not the one in the corner, I want the booth more centrally located, near the window"

Everyone was called sweetie by Mrs. Michaels. It eliminated the need for personalization. The apprehensive and slightly

1

confused hostess led Mrs. Michael's procession to the centrally located window booth.

Eager to seat the menacing Mrs. Michaels the hostess gestured toward the empty booth awaiting Mrs. Michaels' approval. Mrs. Michaels gave a quick visual inspection of the booth and proceeded to sit

"yes this will do, please have our waiter take our beverage order immediately."

"Of course Mrs. Michaels, Your waiter is Jorge and I will tell him you are here" she sighed deeply as she turned away and retreated from the table. Within seconds Mrs. Michaels started to complain

"Damn, where's that waiter? All I've done today is hurry up and wait" looking to her companion Mrs. Michaels continued

"Sweetie, I'm parched, Do you remember the waiters name? I come here all the time and I never seem to see the same wait staff twice, always new help - In my opinion it reeks of poor management..." Her voice drifted off as she redirected her focus to the menu

"The food is acceptable, actually quite palatable, for this side of town... the quality of the food makes up for the poor service and unskilled staff..." Just as she finished her rant their server Jorge appeared. Jorge was tall and lanky with chiseled features and a friendly smile

"Good afternoon Mrs. Michaels, you are looking well...'" somewhat annoyed with Jorge's cheerful and potentially insincere greeting Mrs. Michaels interrupted him and responded "yes, yes, yes, I'm as well as ever ...so Sweetie, please fetch us each a Long Island Ice tea while we peruse the menu" Mrs. Michaels cast her glance back to the menu only to hear the voice of her companion speak up

"Excuse me, but if it's no trouble I'd prefer an unsweetened ice tea instead" with a scrutinizing eye Mrs. Michaels turned her attention to correcting her companion "You DO mean a Long Island Ice tea, yes? Or perhaps a glass of wine?" Confidently, yet politely her companion responded "No, an unsweetened ice tea, please". Jorge nodded and scurried off to retrieve their respective drinks. Unaccustomed to being contradicted Mrs.

Michaels took new notice of her seemingly coy companion as she thought to herself, "Perhaps this girl is spunkier than she appears". As quickly as the thought passed thru Mrs. Michaels mind she just as quickly dismissed it, and returned to reading the menu. Jorge stealthily delivered the drinks and disappeared into a sea of waiters.

Mrs. Michaels' companion appeared docile and unassuming. Dressed conservatively yet stylishly she appeared confident yet not overbearing. She was pleasant whereas Mrs. Michaels was ominous. She carried herself with the self assurance of someone who knows who they are and where they fit into the world yet without the arrogance and blatant egotism of Mrs. Michaels.

Mrs. Michaels' was ready to place her order and began to fidget impatiently as she looked around for Jorge. Drinking her Long Island Ice tea as if it were water she started speaking in louder tones.

"Where is that waiter? When you don't need them they hover around like buzzards and when you want one they vanish.. .Sweetie? (Looking at her companion) Do you remember his name? "

Mrs. Michaels' companion responded "I believe his name is Jorge".

"Jorge? No, that isn't it; I would remember that, it was something else, something exotic…"

"Yes, I am certain it is Jorge" Mrs. Michaels' companion confidently stated.

"Well, where the hell is he? I need another drink and we need to order!! Just as Mrs. Michaels finished her drink a waiter from another section of the restaurant passed by Mrs. Michaels' booth and with impeccable timing Mrs. Michaels grabbed his arm and began her very public reprimand "We have been waiting hours for you to take our order and to fetch us another round of drinks, I have never had as poor service as I have at this restaurant"

The waiter looked puzzled and very perplexed as he shook free from her grasp and responded "I'll get your server ma'm ". Mrs. Michaels looked frustrated and increasingly more impatient "You can't take our order? Do you know who I am? "Still

3

perplexed the waiter answered "Yes Mrs. Michaels, I know who you are and I will gladly get your waiter for you". Fortunately, Jorge reappeared almost instantly with a fresh Long Island Ice Tea for Mrs. Michaels and an unsweetened ice tea for her companion. Jorge quickly wrote down their food requests and slyly made his escape. For the moment Mrs. Michaels was pacified.

With one hand continually wrapped around her glass, and the other hand clutching her fork Mrs. Michaels methodically would eat one bite of food and follow it with a swallow of beverage. Mrs. Michaels' companion was unfazed by Mrs. Michaels' idiosyncrasies and ate her meal in a much more leisurely manner. The ladies exchanged polite conversation as they ate their meals. Throughout the meal, Mrs. Michaels kept a watchful eye on Jorge keeping him busy refilling and retrieving her Long Island Ice Teas. Eventually Mrs. Michaels was saturated with Long island Ice Tea. At this point Mrs. Michaels directed her attention to her companion while continuing to keep one hand wrapped around the glass and an eye on Jorge.
"So, what is the real reason I have the privilege of your company today? It's quite a rarity that my brother actually sends someone to consult with me" "Did the stock market crash?? Or perhaps he misappropriated my funds and has left the country..?" hummmm "Let me guess, you must be a stockbroker in training? No, you'd be wearing Prada if you were any kind of stockbroker!!! HA HA HA " Mrs. Michaels seemed to be entertaining herself delivering a soliloquy for the benefit of her companion and anyone else who was interested in listening to her. Her voice kept getting louder and less audible and other restaurant patrons appeared uncomfortable with her rant. Mrs. Michaels' companion, who had said very little up to this point began to speak. Completely unfazed by Mrs. Michaels' disparaging remarks her companion began to speak in very soothing and yet restrained tones
"As you know, I do work for your brother, as well as your ex-husband. They both care for you deeply and have very serious concerns regarding your health and well being" Mrs. Michaels interrupted her companion, furious to hear mention of her ex

husband. Her rant was now not only against her brother but her ex husband as well.

"Tell me, are they working together now? ? Sneering, and seething Mrs. Michaels continued to shout at her well composed companion. "Ha, not only politics makes odd bed fellows but so does divorce…" now, was contorting her face in the most unattractive smirk while slurring her words which were becoming increasingly sarcastic. Mrs. Michaels went on.

"So what do these caring gentlemen have planned for me? "Mrs. Michaels' glared at her companion, daring her to continue. Calmly and coolly, ignoring the tirade she went on to explain the plan.

"They have decided to stop your monthly allowance unless you agree to go into a long term addictions rehabilitation facility" " They have reason to believe you are squandering your wealth and will not have any money left by the time you are of retirement age if they do not help you now". "Your brother has provided me with an excel spread sheet of your expenses for the last six months and this letter which he has asked me to read to you, may I?" Mrs. Michaels nodded to her companion totally disgusted with the conversation yet curious as to what else her brother could have in store for her. Mrs. Michael's companion began;

"My Dear Sister,

It is with great sadness that I am writing this note. Your finances have become noticeably unmanageable as is your drinking. As your financial advisor and brother I need to take action now to protect your financial interests and your health before you have exhausted both. Please examine the enclosed excel spread sheet. I found several points worth noting. First, it shows your increasing financial assistance to the liquor industry. I can confidently state that you, my dear sister, Mrs. Michaels, have single handedly restored an industry that previously was on a decline but through your tenacious consumption, one drink at a time, you can be credited with saving a floundering industry." Mrs. Michaels snickered at the obvious sarcastic tone but continued to listen.

Secondly, your daily choice of alcohol before family and friends has alienated everyone who has ever cared for you. I, for one can not remember the last time you uttered a kind word to any of us. Finally, your liver, kidneys and entire digestive system scream out for an entire cleansing, not to mention a memorial to sacrificed brain cells, which has defied sobriety." Mrs. Michaels' companion's tone changed, becoming gentle and almost soothing as she gave the impression she was concluding

"Let me state once again, It is because we love and care for you, and want you to live a long prosperous life that we need to take action now, Please consider this request. Your loving brother."

Mrs. Michaels glared at her companion; her eyes seemed to turn black with rage as her jaw was clutched shut, her chin jetted forward. Mrs. Michaels' companion had stopped speaking and became silent. The restaurant seemed to become equally silent as Mrs. Michaels rose out of her seat, like a phoenix rising out of the ashes, her glass in hand, and in her loudest most arrogant voice she turned to her companion and screamed a scream that seemed to well up from the very core of her being "Sweetie, DO YOU KNOW WHO I AM????? There is NO WAY, do you hear me? NO WAY you, my brother, my ex husband or one hundred ex husbands will EVER stop my allowance or put me away!!! How many conversations with how many associates must I endue to make it clear – I AM NOT going to rehab!! DO YOU UNDERSTAND? It is MY money and I will spend it however I choose. Damn, where is that waiter?? What did you say his name is??" Jorge resurfaced before anyone could respond. Seeing Jorge seemed to put Mrs. Michaels slightly more at ease as she regained her composure and sat back down. Somewhat relieved and seemingly rescued by the presence of Jorge, she made her final request of the brow beaten waiter "Sweetie, Get me another Long Island Ice Tea … And the check… now. " Mrs. Michaels' companion sat very quietly, watching as Mrs. Michaels instantly downed her drink; her rant had finished and as far as she was concerned the issue was mute. For Mrs. Michaels it was business as usual.

"What the caterpillar calls the end of the world,
the master calls a butterfly."

—Richard Bach

False Start

*J*ust as the interview was about to begin, Olivia requested a cigarette. Not being a smoker, but wanting my client to be comfortable, I sought out a cigarette from a gentleman in the next room. Presenting it to Olivia, she took it, placed it between her lips and lite it with the ease of someone who had lit a million before this one. Inhaling deeply and sitting back in her chair she politely asked "Where do you want to start?" Prepared to give her some direction I matter of factly suggested she start at the beginning. A serious, let's get this over with; look crossed her face as she began. "My life drinking is nothing to brag 'bout." "Alcohol was always part of my life so I didn't think anything was wrong with it". Slowly exhaling the smoke and watching it dissipate; Olivia continues "Same with fighting, cussing, and moving."

From the time she was a very small child, Olivia's family seemed to always be moving. "It was my Mother, my older sister, Karee, my Dad, and me. My mother bragged that she could have us packed up and ready to leave, any place, in less than an hour". And less than an hour it was, "Usually after a fight with the landlord, a neighbor or Dad, and usually after she had been

7

drinking'". Ironically, Olivia never blamed her mother's use of alcohol as part of the problem she just figured she had a bad mother.

Olivia's mother drank everyday, some days less than others but everyday just the same. Olivia was lucky her sister Karee was home when she was little to at least start her off to school but Karee was 4 years older than Olivia and she left home for good when Olivia was 10. "I missed Karee terribly and I hated being alone with my mom". Karee never came back and Olivia felt abandoned by the one person she trusted to care for her. "The days and nights were all the same". "Mom drank and fought with whoever was around and would finally pass out. I felt as if I was always alone and I hated it." Olivia became quiet and pensive when asked about her Dad. After some thought Olivia replied "Dad was not home much and no one said why. When he did come home he made me feel like the most special person in the world, and then he would leave, usually after a fight with mom. I never knew when I'd see him again. I was angry with him for not being home and I was angry because I had to stay with Mom".

Just like her sister Karee, Olivia could not wait to leave home. She started waitressing when she was 15-yrs-old at a local diner where she would work as late as possible as to avoid going home. The owner, an elderly cantankerous woman who seldom had a kind word but respected Olivia's work ethic would let Olivia stay and sleep on a cot in a back room. "If I woke in time I'd go to school, if not I'd work another shift" Inhaling deeply on the cigarette, Olivia continued "I eventually dropped out of school and just worked as much as possible, I'd do anything not to be home". Exhale rings of smoke " I have always hated being alone, and being with my mother was like being alone - she was always drunk or hung over - I wanted a real home and a family". Olivia's gaze became lifeless as she seemed to fall into a trance like state, staring into empty space "work became my life at 15-years old".

It wasn't long after Olivia dropped out of school that she met Johnnie. Johnnie was a tall handsome truck driver. He had a quick smile and a friendly manner. Olivia liked the gentle way he talked to everyone. She was 16, he was 24; they married six months later, mostly at Olivia's insistence. Johnnie had a big family, the kind of family Olivia thought she wanted-complete with several brothers and sisters, lots of cousins, aunts and uncles and all drinkers. "I married into a family of drinkers but I didn't care because I now had a real family and I would never be alone. Boy was I wrong".

Johnnie worked as an "over the road" truck driver. He was gone 2 or 3 weeks at a time.

Johnnie didn't drink when he was on the road but liked to drink when he was home. Olivia was amused that when Johnnie drank he would just fall asleep. So, when he came home, whether he had been drinking, or not, he would sleep. The newlyweds had a small, two room, 5th floor, walk-up apartment. The hub for his truck (and their home) was 60 miles away from all family so once again Olivia was alone. It seemed like no matter where she went she was always alone. At night every little sound frightened Olivia and she feared someone was braking in - "That's when I started drinking; vodka, was my first choice - it was cheep and I didn't need much". "Vodka eased the loneliness and helped me sleep". At first I couldn't stand the taste, it burned as it went down, but I could mix it with just about anything. After awhile I got use to it and could drink it straight". Olivia justified her drinking by telling herself she would only drink at night, to help her sleep and forget how much she missed Johnnie.

After saying that, she smirked as she confessed to needing a drink in the morning to help get started. "Sometimes my head hurt so badly I could barely move. Just a sip of vodka seemed to make that pain go away". It wasn't too long till Olivia chose to stop working at the diner cause she could not keep her hands from shaking and she feared she would drop something on someone. She also feared someone would smell the alcohol on her breath. Another deep inhale on the cigarette as she thoughtfully paused, "plus, Johnnie was making good money so why should I work?" One year into the marriage Olivia found out she was pregnant. Exhaling from the cigarette, a smile creeps across Olivia's face as her eyes become distant. "I was so happy." Inhale " I thought I would never be alone again, finally the family I always wanted". Exhale "Johnnie was concerned about my drinking and I agreed to stop drinking Vodka while I was pregnant. I was fine as long as Johnnie was home but when he was out of town I couldn't sleep so I started to drink wine". Chuckling to herself Olivia explained her scientific reasoning for drinking wine instead of vodka when she was pregnant. Olivia explained to me that she had convinced herself "it would be easier to digest wine since wine was from fruit and fruit would be good for the baby". We both laughed at the insanity of her thinking! In reality, Olivia couldn't stand the idea of not drinking, even while pregnant.

Johnnie hated when Olivia drank, he would threaten not to come home if she was drinking, yet that didn't stop her. "I just had to be more clever" she smirk and sneered.

Olivia remembered stocking up during the week when Johnnie was out of town and hid the bottles away, "just in case".

Sometimes she hid them so well she couldn't find them. One time, when she was 3 months pregnant, Johnnie was sick of watching her drink, he took the wine she was drinking and poured it down the drain, as Olivia watched in absolute horror. Tears welled up in Olivia's eyes as she recalled how she yelled at Johnnie "I HATE YOU, I wish I never married you or moved into this God forsaken town". Johnnie grabbed his coat and hat and told Olivia he would do her a favor and leave. Olivia choked back the tears as she continued, "I was so angry; I grabbed the empty bottle and threw it at him, just missing his head, as he went out the door." Inhale deeply "I'll never forget the look he gave me as he continued down the stairs and into his truck, shattered glass everywhere." "I slammed the apartment door and proceeded to tear the place apart looking for another bottle of wine". Exhale "I found one, but passed out before I could open it". Johnnie didn't come home for a month. Johnnie finally called Olivia and she begged him to come back, promising never to drink again; as long as he didn't drink, she wouldn't drink. She promised him everything would be different. "Funny, when I made those promises, I meant them with all my heart, I really did love Johnnie, and I knew he loved me". Johnnie moved back into there home and everything was great for a couple weeks. Olivia boasted of being the perfect wife - for that short time! The next week Johnny was assigned a different, unfamiliar route, knowing Olivia's insecurity, Johnnie called and said he'd be a little later than usual. When Johnnie got home, several hours later he seemed ok but smelt like beer and that set Olivia off. "I figured if he was drinking so would I". "That ended my brief interval of being alcohol free!" So Olivia proceeded to continue drinking wine and Johnnie spent less and less time at home. Finally, the baby was born. Olivia smiles as she thinks about the birth of her baby, "She was tiny, much smaller than the other babies in the hospital and the doctors said she was small because I drank during my pregnancy. I felt so bad that I did this to my child." The cigarette now burned to the filter, dangled from Olivia's now limp hand as she continued, "once again, I made a promise, as long as my baby lived, I would never drink again". The baby was named Sara. Each morning Olivia visited baby Sara at the hospital. She held her and rocked her and sang to her. Each day Sara became stronger and bigger until finally Johnnie and Olivia were able to bring baby Sara home. Olivia looked me straight in the eyes and stated "Finally, I had the family I dreamed of, Johnnie, baby Sara, and me". And then she cried, briefly, as if embarrassed by the show of emotion. Olivia pulled herself together and continued her story.

"Life at home was no picnic. Johnnie was back on the road, and I was home with a crying, colicky baby. Nothing I did would quiet Sara. I was lonely and very sad." Sara was so demanding. After one particularly sleepless night the landlord told Olivia to put a little scotch in Sara's milk bottle to help her sleep cause she was keeping everyone in the building awake. "If it (scotch) is good enough for Sara, it's good enough for me". Wistfully Olivia continued "After all, I wasn't sleeping either. I was lonely, tired, and angry at the world and I wanted a drink"

Motherhood and family life wasn't what Olivia expected. Everyday was the same. Olivia was drinking from dawn to dusk, and so was Sara. Her beautiful two-month-old baby girl became under weight and under nourished. Johnnie was never home. Olivia was miserable when he was gone and she was miserable when he was home. Johnnie couldn't stand to watch her drink so he would work more or just sleep in his truck.

At this point in the interview, Olivia appeared restless and suddenly agitated. I asked if I could get her a soda, maybe coffee, A snack? And she snapped impatiently " how about a cigarette?" I once again sought out another fire stick which she snatched from my hand, placed in her mouth and lit instantly. A deep inhale followed by a deep exhale. She seemed soothed. Leaning closer to me, as if to share a secret, in a very low voice that was almost a whisper, Olivia muttered "My baby Sara died, and it was my fault" Trying not to appear aghast I let her continue, "It was a night that Johnnie wasn't coming home, I was really lonely and the baby was really colicky. It was as if neither of us could be content. I had been giving baby Sara scotch in her milk but that day she seemed extra disturbed so I gave her twice as much. I was angry at Johnnie for not being home, angry with baby Sara for being so demanding; angry with my parents, my neighbors the landlord, with the world, with God, etc etc. I was mostly angry at myself. I crawled into my bed, with baby Sara next to me, my tumbler full of scotch in my right hand and a cigarette in my left. I drank and smoked till I passed out. That night I killed my beautiful baby girl. When I passed out, in bed, with a glass of scotch and a lit cigarette, the blanket caught on fire. I got out, burned and bruised, baby Sara didn't. I forgot all about her as I left her behind, in my burning bed, to die." A deep inhale a deep exhale, the glow of the cigarette burning slowly as Olivia's gaze stayed fixed far far away.

Olivia was arrested and convicted of killing her own child. She was sent to jail and eventually rehab. It was only at this time that she was able to begin work on her new life. Olivia maintained a calm appearance as she continued her story "Right now I haven't drank since July 20, 2004. My thinking is real clear and I feel better (most of the time) about myself and my life. I sometimes cry for my dead baby girl and what her life might have been. I feel sad because so much was wasted. My child is gone, never to return, and so is Johnnie. I can never replace my child or fix my relationship with Johnnie. Jail gave me an appreciation for time and I don't want to waste any more of it." Silently staring into space Olivia continued in a very hushed voice "Jail and rehab gave me a lot of time to think. I have a lot on my mind and sometimes I become overwhelmed: the old feelings of being alone haunt me. Now I realize that being alone is ok. Vodka, Wine or anything alcoholic was my enemy and always will be."

"When I drank I was more alone than ever. Now I use my alone time to think and then do the next right things. I have a sponsor, friends and an AA home group. I go to church, I volunteer at the hospital. When I feel lonely, I go to a meeting or call my sponsor. Sometimes I just shake the urge to use by believing "this too will pass" It's definitely one day at a time. This is no false start"

Petulance and Pomeral

I can't remember exactly when I first met Pete. It was several years ago as we were both substantially younger, perhaps in our late forties, and our meeting was quite accidental. It was raining, and the storm was getting worse, I had been driving for several hours and was looking for a place to get something to eat and drink. I remember veering off the interstate and randomly stopping at the No Name Bar. It looked clean and simple, one neon beer light, adequate parking, not a lot of commercial glitz. I entered and immediately felt at home, the recognizable sound of a juke box and smell of stale beer and cigarettes welcomed me. As a stranger, I cautiously sat at the far end of the bar - never sure how the local regulars would respond to a stranger. Comforted after a long day of driving by the sights, sounds and smells of a bar I eased into my surroundings, ready for some food and a drink.

"What'll it be?" the bartender eagerly asked

"A scotch, make it a double" I replied settling onto my stool, "I've been traveling all day and I could use something to eat - is your kitchen open?"

A voice from the far end of the bar roared "don't eat the burgers, don't know the last time Joe went to the market and I haven't seen Joe's dog in a week!!" A teasing wink and smile to Joe, the bartender, and a friendly "how you doing" from the man with the booming voice...

"I'm fine, just tired and hungry - too much traffic on the interstate for my liking..." my voice trailed off as Joe placed a menu in front of me.

"Just give me a shout when you are ready to order" Joe said as he exited from around the bar and proceeded to redirect his focus on throwing darts. The bar was quiet, just the way I liked it. I perused the menu and sipped my scotch.

"Where you from?" bellowed the same man's voice from across the bar, obviously curious. Picking up his glass and bills from the bar he moved to the stool next to me.

"The name is Pete, Pete Stiles, I live about a half mile down the road" "Lousy day to travel" he said.

Reluctant to give too much information but feeling oddly at ease with this ebullient companion I shared the dull and dreary details of my day -the day in the life of a computer salesman. Pete listened with amazing tenacity, never seeming bored or uninterested. I stopped talking long enough to sip my scotch as Pete summoned the bartender

"Joe, Order my friend here a decent burger, fries and one of those healthy salads you make - spare him Fido ok? " looking back at me "that sound ok? If you don't order soon he'll close up and you won't find anywhere else to eat tonight"

"Sure, sure that sounds fine," I was actually relived not to make a decision. And Pete's choice of local fare was fine. I ordered another round of drinks to which Pete toasted my health and took a long, languishing taste before he swallowed his wine. After eating my burger and finishing my drink we wished each other well and parted, two strangers whose paths accidentally crossed on a stormy night.

Our first meeting would not have been so memorable if it were a once and done stop.

It was several weeks before I was back to the No Name Bar. My work took me from Maine to Florida and it was rare for me to spend much time in any one place. A creature of habit and liking the familiar, I would make a point to always stop at the No Name Bar when I was in that area. And Pete was always there. Pete was not a loner, in fact the only time I ever saw him by himself was the stormy night we first met. After that there was always someone seated on the stool beside him. Pete was an enigma. His energy seemed to fill the room even when he was quiet. Quiet was not the norm for Pete, as I figured out fairly quickly when Pete was around it was never dull. Men and women alike were drawn to him. Men, for his dominating machismo, especially if challenged to arm wrestle or shoot a round of pool. Women too, were impressed by his physical strength and courage, but also his charisma and charm. His smile was easy, his manner was straightforward; there was nothing pretentious or phony about Pete.   Not bad looking or exceptionally good looking, Pete was always neat and clean, yet had a roguish expression that made one wonder if he was up to something mischievous. Pete's hair was prematurely salt and pepper colored and although he needed glasses to read, his eyes were sharp and focused making one think he had the ability to read the person he was looking at. When happy, his eyes laughed, when angry, his eyes were fireballs.   His burly frame and bawdy mannerisms would first impress the unfamiliar that he was a macho bully. His voice could be thunderous, often intimidating when arguing a point and his attitude could appear patronizing.   He spoke of "manly" exploits such as hunting, drinking and womanizing. Yet his behaviors contradicted his speech - although course and sometimes crude he could also be gentle and kind as he always rallied for the underdog. He was boisterous yet thoughtful, often remembering and valuing intimate and personal details, never forgetting a birthday or special occasion. He was a good listener and a great story teller. His laughter was genuine. He found humor in everything, mostly himself. But above all else he enjoyed his wine.

It was never a secret, Pete loved to drink. At first glance one would think nothing of the natural, flowing connection between Pete's hand, the glass, the wine and his mouth. Pete's large frame could be seen sitting at the center of the bar with the ever present glass of wine always close at hand. He moved with grace and ease; confidence and experience. Like an accomplished lover he consumed the wine with an air of self assurance that only years of practice could provide. Savoring each sip he entertained his companions with animated tales of his escapades. Every day seemed to be an adventure for Pete, even the most ordinary of chores seemed exciting.. His deep voice was hypnotic and his rollicking laughter was contagious. Pete's stories mesmerized his companions, endearing him as the undeclared leader.

One particularly memorable visit was several years after I had become a quasi regular at the No Name Bar. I happened to be traveling the interstate not too far from the No Name Bar when, as had become my routine, I decided to stop. It was early spring; one of those random warm days that the sun shines brilliantly through the trees melting the last remaining heaps of plowed snow. I walked in as Joe the bartender looked up from his newspaper and welcomed me. His hearty greeting made me feel instantly at home.

"How ya doing? Haven't seen you in a while...Will it be the usual? Scotch? "

"Yes, please make it a double - yes, it's been a while... I've been traveling less, you know winter isn't the most lucrative time for sales, especially this winter.. Snow. .the economy... you know..." Joe nodded, as he served the scotch I gazed around the mostly empty bar and remarked "Quiet here, where is everyone?"

"Oh they'll be here, it's still a little early" - almost on cue in through the door came Pete. By his side was a local roofer called Fletch, and following several strides behind was a slight, bird like woman named Terry. The men sat at the bar deep in conversation as Terry followed them coyly sitting next to Pete.

"Hey stranger! How the hell are you?" Pete flashed a smile in my direction as he waved to Joe signaling for a drink. "What do I have to do to get a drink??" "In fact, get everyone a drink" Pete was in an unusually outgoing mood - seemingly half tanked so early in the day. Looking to Terry who hadn't said a word, Pete appeared less bold as he spoke

"You want something to drink, honey?" "If you're hungry order something..."

Terry spoke up looking at Joe, "I'll just have a beer".

Terry was no stranger to the No Name Bar - or any name bar for that matter. Terry was tiny in stature but could be a handful

when drinking. On several previous occasions I had the opportunity to see her in action. It was nothing for her to call out
someone twice her size for disagreeing with her. She could
curse like a trucker and fight like George Foreman. She was
totally unreasonable when drunk. Sober, she was a mouse,
almost socially backward. Seeing Pete with Terry was odd. Pete
liked the ladies and they liked him. Companionship was not a
problem for Pete and Terry was someone Pete would choose
only if there were no other options. The years had not been kind
to Terry and although younger than Pete she looked hard and
tough. She didn't smile much; maybe she had nothing to smile
for, or I would guess because she was conscious of several missing teeth. She often waved a hand in front of her face when she
talked and very rarely looked directly at the person she was talking to. Being seen with Pete was flattering for Terry and really
didn't make any sense to anyone who knew them. Like I said, it
was unusual; no it was just plain weird, to see Terry and Pete
together. Both were known to be volatile when drunk, Terry and
Pete were a dangerous combination. Everyone knew it was best
when they would go their separate ways because of their
propensity for quarreling when drunk. Terry, became drunk
very quickly impart because of her slight size and impart for her
low tolerance for alcohol. Pete, claimed never to get drunk, had
a high tolerance for alcohol and could appear to drink endlessly
until suddenly, with no warning, he would snap and go from
charming and funny to mean and cruel.

Terry, who had now consumed several bottles of beer in a
fairly short period of time, was becoming more verbose. "Pete?
You have any change for the juke box? Pete, PETE?" Pete was
deep in conversation with Fletch regarding the proper pitch for
a dutch roof style as opposed to the pitch for a gabled style roof.
"PETE?" not even casting a glance in Terry's direction, Pete
responded mechanically, "No, I don't have any change" and
continued talking to Fletch. Terry, distracted for the moment by
someone shooting pool ended her pursuit of loose change.
Pete and Fletch were now getting louder as they argued as to the
proper pitch for their project. Just as it became apparent that a
compromise was impossible raucous laughter preceded the

entrance of three more of Pete's cronies who came barreling
into the bar.

"Hey Joe, Good to see you man, how about a round of
drinks for everyone?" With drink chips adding up in front of
me and still slowly nursing my first scotch I could see this turning into a long day into night. Terry, very aware that she was the
only woman in the bar, and quickly becoming inebriated, took
on an air of self-assurance and confidence not seen two hours
earlier. Now poised and perched on a stool near the pool table
she attempted to flirt with a quiet, queerly dressed man shooting pool. With no tact she would look longingly at Pete hoping
for even a remote sign of jealousy, but he couldn't care less. The
less he cared the more she drank and the more annoyed she
became at his lack of interest in her. Terry proceeded to throw
herself at the man playing pool, who was strangely sober, and
did not have any interest in her. Feeling rejected Terry resumed
her focus on Pete. "Peeeeeete PEEEEEETE, I want to dance,
come dance with me..... Pete...." Terry's whining voice echoed
through the bar - Pete, already over whatever connection they
shared earlier, looked disgusted and did not acknowledge her
whining. Not happy to be relegated to unknown status Terry
continued to assert herself. Pete, entertained by the company of
Fletch, the three cronies, the quiet, queerly dressed pool shooting man, and myself, gave no thought to Terry. Terry pushed her
way through the group of men talking to Pete and attached herself to his arm stating emphatically, "I SAID, I want to dance,
NOW, with you..." loosing her footing while trying to place it
on the bar rail, Terry spilt the beer she was drinking directly on
Pete's lap. Pete flew into a rage "What the Hell is the matter
with you, dumb bitch, Get the hell away from me -one roll in
the hay and you think we're a couple? Ha, this is why I never
got married..... "The stunned on lookers became quiet, unsure
of which direction Pete's rage could turn.   Terry, now drunk,
humiliated and full of anger, was not going to let Pete have the
last word. "Who the hell do you think you are??   George
Clooney? Brad Pitt? You're just an old drunk" Terry was now
nose to nose with Pete, screaming in each others faces.   Joe
finally stepped in, ordering Terry to go sit down at a table and

cagily suggested to Pete that he should rinse his beer soiled pants. Pete, still cursing Terry, stomped off into the men's room to wash up. Conscious not to be heard by Pete, his soiled pants became the brunt of jokes as the group burst into laughter... When he returned, the laughter stopped. Pete resumed his place at the bar, next to Fletch, and before saying a word reached for his glass, placed his lips on the rim and took a long, satisfying swallow of wine. His eyes closed, his hands around the glass, he savored the taste of the wine and remarked, "I love wine, I REALLY Love Wine" and without further delay continued discussing the roof's pitch with Fletch. Terry, drinking at a table by herself, kept her distance from Pete until he was ready to leave. With a tone of finality Pete announced "well that's all I have to say about that!" as he Bid farewell to Fletch, the three cronies, the quiet, queerly dressed pool shooting man, and I, Pete stumbled to the exit. Almost as an after thought, he turned around looked at Terry and asked her "Well, are you coming or not? You old whore, don't be so difficult..." looking pleased and peculiarly flattered, Terry staggered to Pete's side and away they went.

It was quite a few years after that incident that I returned to the No Name Bar. Pete was there, at the center of the bar, his glass of wine close at hand as he chatted amicably with other patrons. . The years appeared to have taken their toll on Pete. His hair was now more salt than pepper colored and thinning. His demeanor was less outgoing and more stoic. He raised his glass and smiled in my direction as I seated myself at the opposite side of the bar. I noticed a dark haired woman seated next to Pete who seemed very familiar yet I could not remember her name. Over time many women seemed to come and go through Pete's life. Some were more memorable than others, none ever lasting. I often wondered if it was by his choice or theirs that such a social man was ultimately alone. As the other patrons cleared out Pete collected his money and his glass from the bar as he moved to the stool next to me. "Hey Bud, how you doing? Haven't seen you in ages..." His eyes deeply locked onto mine, waiting for my response "I'm good, work could be better but I can't complain" "How you doing Pete?" "You ok?" "Oh yeah, sure, couldn't be better - Where are my manners, you remember Diane don't you? She use to work here..." now it came back to me, of course, she was a bartender. Diane and I exchanged civilities as she announced it was time to go. She hugged Pete, told him to take care and she'd see him around. And away she went. Pete appeared pensive as she left, focusing his attention on his wine. Breaking the silence I comment "She seems well".

Sipping his wine Pete replied with no enthusiasm "Yeah, she's a good girl; she'll be leaving after the week-end"

"You planning to see her again?" I was feeling an unusual urge to play match maker as well as wanting to see Pete with someone nice "Don't you ever think of settling down?" Realizing that I was probably over stepping the boundaries of barroom etiquette I took the chance and continued "You're a fun, smart guy, don't you ever think about having a home life instead of a bar life? You know one woman, a home, maybe a yard and a dog......" "Yeah Yeah, sure I think about it but the time for housekeeping is done - I'm pushing 60-years-old ...."Pete's voice trailed off as he seemed to be daydreaming about days long gone. "I once was in love with a great girl, MaryAnn, She was spunky and beautiful and we were young" he continued" Never knew anyone like her - now or then... I could've easily spent the rest of my life with her and I thought we would except I was young and stupid" Pete stopped talking, as if to catch himself before divulging too much. He cleared his throat and ordered another glass of wine. Joe, who was playing darts, served up the wine then returned to his game, paying no attention to the serious conversation between me and Pete. "MaryAnn was the kind of girl you marry and have kids with - she didn't hang out in places like this, she had too much going on.... I wanted to marry her and she wanted to marry me but I messed up - big time and she left me... I've never known another woman like her; she was one of a kind..and that's all I have to say about that." I didn't say anything, I sipped my scotch and he sipped his wine, curious to ask what he did but realizing it didn't matter, Time doesn't heal everything, and sometimes, like it seemed for Pete, time just stops as life passes you by. I wanted to tell Pete it was ok, that he'd meet someone else but I knew the words were shallow. Almost forty years have gone by, Mary Ann never came back and Pete never forgot. Women have come and gone, none filling the void left by one woman, so many years before. Whatever it was that broke the relationship no longer mattered, the pain was as fresh as if it happened yesterday. We both felt the uncomfortable seriousness of the moment as Pete piped up "Nothing compares to a fine glass of wine" Pete raised his glass -" here's to you Bud, and here's to fine wine!!!" savoring the taste of the wine as if inhaling fresh air Pete rebounded into the present "How about a game of darts? Joes's been warming up all afternoon - ready to be challenged Joe? Ha!" One more sip of wine and Pete was on his feet, and the game was on!

> *'A Man who removes a mountain begins*
> *by carrying away small stones"*
> —Chinese Proverb

The Lonely Life of
Randolph Edgar Dertinger

My earliest memory was when I was four-years-old, chasing after other children at the pre-school. The other kids would come and go throughout the day as I would always be the first child dropped off in the morning and the last one picked up at night. Being an only child, my parents were my world. Although a timid child I enjoyed the company of other kids. I would watch them while I would wait eagerly for my parents to finish work and retrieve me. I was just one more scheduled stop in their daily routine.

My parents met at a fraternity party at the college they both were attending. They would boost that theirs was the perfect love story; "they met, fell in love and were married".

As perfect as their romance, were their careers. When they graduated from college the same investment firm hired both of them immediately. Their lives were perfect; they loved their work, they loved each other and everyone loved them, life was perfect– and then along came me. I can remember hearing my father entertaining anyone who would listen with his explanation of my existence by stating that I was the result of "defective birth control". I grew up feeling like the punch line to my father's cruel jokes. My mother was distant and cold, never one to randomly hug or show affection to anyone – including my father and me. Even when she ceremoniously would kiss me I was instructed not to mess her hair, smear her make-up or wrinkle her clothes. I felt like an accessory to her posh and polished façade. We were the picture of perfection. One of the few perks of being an only child (of emotionally void parents), was getting what I wanted when I wanted it. There was no delayed gratification. My parents found it easier to give me whatever I wanted, as a way of silencing me. This exchange worked for all of us. I played the role of the happy child, smiling and dutifully falling into place and they had the picture perfect family - until I turned thirteen. At thirteen-years of age, as a matter of protocol, I went to boarding school, "The" Edgewood Cliffs Academy. My parents were on the fast track with successful careers and busy lives that did not include time for hands on parenting. I had all the "things" that made it appear that my life was ok yet I was sad and very lonely. All the while living with my parents I felt alienated and distanced emotionally, I never felt wanted or valued, yet when the time came to leave I still did not want to go. I begged, cried, and pleaded to stay but they had made their minds up. I had tried so long and so hard to be perfect, to fit into their lives without causing any discord I could not imagine why I was being sent away. In my very immature 13-year-old brain I was being sent to some far off land, Siberia perhaps? - somewhere to be forgotten. I held back the tears, took a deep breath and packed my bag. My mother reminded me that the driver was waiting and it was time to leave. Indifferent to my staying or going my mother watched me pack, more concerned with the procedure of packing than my oblivious emotional distress. After a stoic good bye and handshake from my father and an obligatory kiss on the cheek for my mother off I went, to school in New England and to my new, separate life.

The Edgewood Cliffs Academy presented many new opportunities. In the classroom, I felt confident and superior to my peers. Educationally I was above average yet challenged by the high standard of the curriculum. School still came easy to me. Outside the classroom was a different story. I was socially uncomfortable; a geek. I found it difficult to get close to anyone. The façade of perfection and intellectualism that I had learned to wear as a child cloaked me well as I grew up. People only knew what I allowed them to know about me. And that was minimal. I had many acquaintances but no real friends. The first person I met at boarding school was my roommate, James Jay Pennyworth, who liked to be called JJ. JJ was my polar opposite, friendly and outgoing with a smile that glistened perfect sparkling white teeth from ear to ear.

"Hey man" he confidently roared across the room sure to get my attention. Cautiously I responded "hey" with considerable less enthusiasm.

"What's your name?" I sheepishly said "Randolph", hoping that would be the end of our conversation but he continued "hummmm, you have a middle name?

"Edgar". "what?" I repeated "Edgar" more emphatically. JJ looked at me as if he were trying to figure something out "Your last name is Dertinger ...right? I nodded wondering where this interrogation was heading when finally JJ announced

"I'm going to call you Red - get it? Randolph Edgar Dertinger - Red!! "JJ grinned his mile wide toothy smile and appeared quite pleased with himself, still muttering Red under his breath with the same satisfaction as if he answered the finale daily double jeopardy million dollar question. Feeling a bit light headed and unsure if the conversation or company caused my unsteadiness I headed out the door, catching a passing whiff of JJ - JJ reeked of expensive cologne, worn with customary schoolboy enthusiasm. I was soon to learn that there was never an opportunity not to wear cologne. Quite the showman, JJ would entertain his less worldly peers with stories of exotic travels and famous people. To the less educated ear he seemed fascinating; to the better read/educated person he seemed boastful and full of himself. Rather than feed JJ's insatiable ego by joining the ever growing group of JJ wanna be's, I preferred to hide in my books and studies, video games, and occasionally smoke weed.

Days and week-ends at The Edgewood Cliff Academy blended together, as did the months and years. I grew to prefer week days when school was in session to when there were more people around to week-ends and holidays. At first weekends and holidays were often disappointing because many of my peers would be going home or on some sort of family vacation – but not me. For my parents to actually bring me home or visit with me was a rarity. A benefit to rooming with the gregarious JJ was that JJ always went somewhere, leaving me to be alone and that was not a bad thing. I enjoyed my time alone, reading or playing video games. My parents would religiously e-mail me Friday afternoons, always glib, always light hearted. More times than not, an apology and an expensive gift would have to suffice for their company. Happy with their work, happy with each other, happy I was at school. Minimally interested in me, I learned not to expect anything from my parents. My parent's responsibility was to pay my tuition and keep spending money in my account, anything more than that was a fluke My role was to occasionally embellish their lives then go away. I was hurt, angry and very resentful. "I would rhetorically ask "How could such shallow people have me as their son?" Sometimes it was so painful to think about I would look for any escape.

On one exceptionally dismal week-end another classmate and casual acquaintance, Tim Hastings, appeared in my building. An odd fellow, with an ability to appear much older than his 15 years, his tall slim frame always appeared hunched forward. His dark hair was tussled and his eyes were narrowly set with sparse scruffy stray whiskers on his upper lip giving the appearance of a rodent. When you least expected to see him he seemed to materialize, this time offering me a bag of weed and his dime store advice " don't look so glum, kick back, roll a fat one and relax", he continued "I got something special for you" Tim looked very uncomfortable as he kept transferring his weight from one foot to the other, his hands awkwardly rubbing together as if he was washing them, never letting go of the bag of weed. Tim was a reliable source of weed - transactions were always short and sweet - no meaningless conversation just a cut and dried business transaction.   I handed him 3 crisp new

$20.00 not listening as Tim restated more emphatically " I put something special in your bag" I suspiciously questioned Tim "What are you talking about? "" I just wanted weed" Tim responded" Chill out! Just some dope, you've never had anything like it- sound good? After all, what'll it hurt? No one gets hooked using it just once, it's my gift to you, enjoy!" Then with a sheepish grin he handed me the bag, and several round tablets. I looked at him questioningly wondering what the pills where but said nothing. I took the bag, politely accepted his gift and watched him walk away. "A lot less fanfare than JJ" I thought as Tim's slim frame vanished into the shadows. I proceeded to look for rolling papers as I swallowed the pills.

By my last year at The Edgewood Cliff Academy, I was smoking pot daily and swallowing 3 or 4 Oxy's daily. I kept to myself, as I always did, going thru the motions of living. I knew my time at The Edgewood Cliff Academy was nearing the end and I was unsure of life after graduation. I was reluctant to move on to college. I had comfortable customs and regular routines at school. Even life with JJ had become doable. I had many reservations about leaving the school that had become my home, and the familiar people and surroundings that were now my life. I secretly clung to the common comforts I knew. The prospect of attending college and beginning another life changing move seemed overwhelming. Yet I dutifully applied and was accepted to several schools - unsure of what I would study but very aware that I needed to move on to this next phase of life.

College was very similar to boarding school – I adjusted to the classes and routine without any problem but once again, the social aspect was difficult. I kept to myself, befriending no one. Once again, marijuana helped ease the strain and tension. Weed became my very best friend and one consistent companion. Initially I smoked just to take the edge off – but soon I found myself smoking before any and all events. Before breakfast, lunch and dinner; before classes, after classes it did not matter. I humored myself by labeling myself a "functional addict". The Oxy's were also part of my daily ritual. Fortunately Tim was still a short drive from campus and was able to supply me with both. My world was very limited, very little else mattered to me. Accustomed to being alone, I had no close friends. I envied people who were naturally comfortable in a group, able to laugh and converse effortlessly, and not need weed or anything else to be social. The Oxy's made me sleepy and I would nod out in class - if I made it to class at all. My grades dropped and I barely went to class. The sad part was that no one seemed to notice. The Friday afternoon e-mails from my parents had long become a charade of meaningless, inconsequential prattle. E-mails were a safe, non-personal way to maintain the appearance of caring. And such remained my family life. Still feeling lonely, emotionally wounded and abandoned, I'd pop another Oxy and let the waves of nothingness wash over me.

As finals approached and my graduation was seriously questionable, my faculty advisor required a meeting with me. We had met previously when it was necessary to have my course selection approved but in my usual manner I avoided any close or lasting contact. I had become quite skilled at making no impression as a first impression. A lasting impression was impossible. Dr. Abrams was a soft talking thoughtful man who carefully and deliberately chose each word and phrase before saying it. Looking me straight in the eye he asked 'what the hell are you doing?" Trying to do my best to look like a sober person, I retorted "nothing", as I attempted to look indignant at his line of questioning. He said "You look awful, your grades are awful, and you're lying". Frantic to escape this unwelcome confrontation I excused myself and bolted for the door. I ran down the hall and onto the down stairwell, loosing my footing, stumbling and turning my ankle. "Damn it! Managing to get out of the building, now limping badly, I reached deep into my pocket, looking for an Oxy but couldn't find one. Panic set in at the prospect of not having any escape. Groping through my pockets now searching for my cell phone I realized I must have dropped it on the stairwell. Knowing I needed my phone to call Tim for more pills, I stealthy slunk back to the stairwell, dragging my injured, now swelling ankle behind me. I held the hand rail while scanning the stairs for my missing phone. As I scrutinized each tread desperately looking for my phone, I was face to face with Dr. Abrams. My heart sank. The throbbing in my ankle, the craving for an Oxy, the despair in my soul, all collided together. The gig was up.

My life was a lie. I was lying to myself. I wanted to believe that everything was ok, that I wasn't miserable and I didn't need weed or drugs. But that wasn't the truth. I had been hiding and lying for as long as I remember. Feelings were pushed aside just as I was pushed aside as a small child. As I looked into this kind man's face, a man who did not know me but knew everything about me. I welled up with tears and sobbed. I cried for the child that was lost, the adolescent that was pushed aside and the young adult who was hiding. I wanted to light up a big fat joint and watch all these feelings go up in smoke.

Yet, another part of me knew the smoke would never taste as sweet. I agreed to go to the hospital for detox - Dr. Abrams stayed with me - silently supporting my sobriety. It was that day and that man that introduced me to society. When I was detoxed and discharged Dr. Abrams was there to take me home. As we left the hospital parking lot Dr Abrams said "I want you to meet some friends of mine, do you mind if we make a stop before you go home?" I agreed, feeling content and passive. We drove a short distance when we pulled into a church parking lot. I felt somewhat anxious as I had never been religious and was not comfortable around religious people. Dr. Abrams got out of the car and simply motioned to me to come along. I nodded and followed him into the basement of the church. It was here I was introduced to Narcotics Anonymous a fellowship of men and women who used and abused drugs the same way I did. For the first time in my life, I felt as if I really belonged somewhere. At first, I just listened. Sure, some of the stories made me uncomfortable but I kept coming back. I found comfort in hearing what they had to say. Eventually I found the courage to talk about myself. People seemed to want to listen and seemed interested in what I had to say and who I was. These were the people I envied, these were people who were comfortable in a group, able to laugh and converse effortlessly, and not need weed or anything else to be social.

I returned to school and found myself becoming more motivated and involved.

Finally, I graduated college, with Dr. Abrams in the front row and marijuana in my past.

Once I was able to make a connection with someone who was interested in me for being just me –not the smart one or the perfect one, I was then able to care about myself and others. The fellowship of NA became the family I never had.

"Things do not change; we change."

—Henry David Thoreau

Till Death do us Part

$\mathcal{M}$onday morning calls to an outpatient drug and alcohol facility are seldom good news. No one ever calls to say they" had a great week-end, the family is sober and we enjoyed each others company, in fact we enjoyed it so much we just had to call and tell you." The reality is that more often the phone rings at 9:01 like it did on Mary's first day soloing as the front desk receptionist. She barely had time to hang her coat and get seated at her desk as the phone rang. She eagerly and very enthusiastically answered it.

"Good morning you have reached Recovery Resources and this is Mary, how can I help you?" Only silence on the other end as Mary hesitated then spoke again "Hello??"

From the silence a frail voice paused than cleared her throat and began

"Oh ah hem... My name is Kelsey Edwards and I'm calling for my husband, Dave, I don't need help (nervous chuckle) HE does, I mean, HE has a drinking problem. He drinks everyday and it's getting worse, in fact I don't know how much more I'm going to be able to take.

"Hello Mrs. Edwards," Mary spoke with a steady, calming tone" is your husband there? It's really best if I speak directly to him."

Mrs. Edwards rebounded with new confidence as she resumed the conversation "oh no he's at work, did I mention he

31

works every day? He's a very hard worker, in fact he never misses work but when he finishes he always stops at the club for a drink before he comes home. I know, I know everyone tells me it's his right, after all he works hard all day and needs to unwind before he comes home..." Kelsey Edwards voice trailed off as Mary spoke up, "Mrs. Edwards? Hello? Mrs. Edwards are you ok? Hello?

"Yes, I'm here, Maybe this wasn't sure a good idea, I really just want an appointment for him to be assessed, maybe he's not a drunk maybe I'm just over reacting..."

Mary interrupted "I really need to speak to your husband, could you have him call back?"

"Oh no, (nervous chuckle) I make all his appointments."

"Mrs. Edwards, I think it would be best if your husband would call to make his own appointment and answer some brief questions."

Mrs. Edwards became alarmed "what kind of questions? I know everything you need to know about him, I can answer all your questions right now, that way he won't be bothered, I really hate to bother him".

Mary calmly answered, "I'm sorry, that's not our policy, I really need to talk to him"

"Fine, I'll tell him." CLICK

She hung up the phone leaving Mary speechless, but unflustered as she continued with other work responsibilities. It was at the very end of the day when Mrs. Edwards resurfaced. Just as Mary was preparing to leave, the phone rang. Eager to make a great first impression her first day on the job, Mary sat back down and answered the phone "Hello, you have reached Recovery Resources and this is Mary, how can I help you?"

"This is Kelsey Edwards, I spoke with you this morning. I have my husband here and he's ready to talk to you, here he is, I'm passing the phone to him now"

"Hello, this is Mary how can I help you?" "Hello?" Mary paused, waiting for Mr. Edwards to speak.

"Yeah, um ahh this is Dave Edwards, I need to make an appointment." The voice sounded guarded and forced.

"Hello Mr. Edwards, I need to ask some questions first to see if you are appropriate for treatment at this facility"

"Hey, I don't need treatment; I just need someone to talk to... How long is this going to take? I'm kind of busy..."

"It will only take a few minutes Mr. Edwards, should I continue?"

"I guess so, is it ok if I put you on speaker phone? My wife wants to hear what's going on".

"Actually, it would be best if I can speak to you alone Mr. Edwards"

"Ok, let me tell her..." Mary turned to her coworker Tammy and shook her head – "These two are attached at the hip!!" Both women shook their heads in disbelief as Mr. Edwards returned to the phone

"She doesn't like it but go ahead – ask your questions".

Mary asked an assortment of questions which all new clients are asked before being accepted into treatment. What is your drug or drink of choice, how often, how much, any legals, any mental health, thoughts of suicide, TB, any other addiction in the family?

Mr. Edwards answered each question succinctly but reluctantly. Mary got to the last question and told Mr. Edwards so "This is the last question, Why do you think you need treatment, err ah, I mean someone to talk to at this time, has something happened to make you want to come here?" Mr. Edwards hesitated, cleared his throat then spoke.

"My wife is the reason. That is, my wife wants me to come there, you know, to talk to someone."

"Oh, ok. Let's set an appointment for someone to assess you, hummmmm how is next Monday at 4:00 pm?'

"Let me ask my wife." He hesitated than responded to Mary

"Yes, that's fine – we'll see you then, Bye"

"Yes, Good bye". Mary hung up the phone, grabbed her coat, said good bye to Tammy and home she went. The rest of Mary's week was uneventful and before she knew it, it was Monday again.

3:15 pm sharp in came Mr. and Mrs. Edwards. Kelsey Edwards was a matronly middle aged woman. Her face looked youthful but it was a safe guess to assume she never smiled. Dave Edwards had a youthful build but his face looked older, rough and aged. His eyes looked sad and sunken. Mrs. Edwards marched directly to Mary and presented her husband, as if he were an erred child.

"I am Kelsey Edwards and this is my husband Dave Edwards" "He has an appointment at 4:00". Mary looked surprised to see both of them so early

"Nice to meet both of you, I'm Mary. Mr. Edwards I have more paperwork for you to fill out before your assessment, do you have your driver's license and insurance card?" With that, Mrs. Edwards sprung into action, "I have both of them", and she proudly stated, "Here is his insurance card and his driver's license." Mary looked shocked – "You carry HIS driver's license? Mrs. Edwards became defensive "of course I do, he looses everything, this way at least one of us knows where things are." Mary, unsure of what to say looked to Tammy for support. Tammy just shook her head and whispered to Mary "she treats him like a 46-year-old baby!!" Mary handed a clipboard to Mr. Edwards with the necessary paperwork for him to fill out but before he was able to take it from Mary, Mrs. Edwards intercepted it.

"I'll take care of this, It's best if I fill it out, He's not good with paperwork.."

Mrs. Edwards had taken over. Mr. Edwards, docile and placated sat down next to his wife as she busied herself with his paperwork. Tammy, who was becoming increasingly less tolerant of the domineering Mrs. Edwards and who has had other experiences with bossy spouses, stepped in for Mary.

"MRS. Edwards, please let your husband fill out the paperwork. We need HIS signature on each page attesting that HE has read and understood each document; perhaps you would like to go next door and get a cup of coffee while he does this?" Mrs. Edwards refused to leave her husband.

"I'm staying with him - incase he needs me" and she sat down next to him determined to stay by his side. Meanwhile, Mr. Edwards appeared very competent filling out his own paperwork. Without any commotion he was able to complete it and hand the finished forms back to Mary. Within minutes an assessment specialist appeared "Mr. Edwards? Is Mr. Edwards here?" Mrs. Edwards spoke up "Here WE are!" The assessment specialist replied "I only need Mr. Edwards right now, but perhaps you would like to go next door and get a cup of coffee while I assess him?" Mrs. Edwards became indignant "I don't drink coffee and I don't want to go next door, I'll wait right here, incase he needs me". She plopped down on the couch and that was that.

Mr. Edwards' assessment was uneventful - when the assessor asked why he wanted an assessment he responded" my wife said I needed one". Further questioning revealed Mr. Edwards was also taking anxiety medication and sleeping pills. He stated he had no intention to stop drinking or using prescription medication. He was only doing this to quiet his wife. The assessor suggested Mr. Edwards just try treatment - perhaps he would find alternative ways to deal with anxiety and his sleep problems. Mr. Edwards was half heartedly willing to give it a try, "after all I don't want to be on pills the rest of my life..." Concluding his assessment Mr. Edwards confidently placed an appointment card in his pocket and a plan in his head. Thinking to himself, he acknowledged, "Maybe this isn't such a bad idea" and joined his wife in the waiting room.

Somewhat relieved that the assessment process was over, Mr. Edwards approached his wife with a big smile as he hugged her and said "I'm starved, let's get out of here" Mrs. Edwards was not as relieved as her husband.

"Where is the lady who assessed him? I have some questions" Mrs. Edwards announced, looking directly at Mary who continued typing, never looking up "She's with another client can I give her a message?" Mr. Edward interrupted her besieging his wife.

"Come on hun, let's get out of here – I have an appointment Wednesday and I can tell you everything else while we eat"

"An Appointment??? Couldn't you have checked with ME first? What if I can't be there? You know how busy I am; you never think about my plans, it's always about you. When are you going to care about what I think or what I have to do?"

Getting impatient Mr. Edwards headed toward the door "I told you, I have an appointment Wednesday, NOT YOU, and I'm hungry NOW, so LET'S GO!! ARE YOU COMING?

Mrs. Edwards plopped back down on the couch. "No, I want to talk to the assessor"

"FINE, sit there and rot there for all I care, I'm getting something to eat and maybe a drink too and the hell with my Wednesday appointment, I'M OUT OF HERE!! And out the door he went. Mary and Tammy continued working, indifferent to the marital tirade.

Mrs. Edwards, looking almost pleased with herself, disdainfully addressed Mary "Don't bother getting the assessor now, I told you he isn't good at making appointments; you should have let ME make the appointment. You made him angry and now he's going to drink. I told you it was getting worse" Gathering her composure, Mrs. Edwards turned her attention to Tammy, "Now he'll NEVER stop drinking and I don't know what to do....I better go find him" and out the door she went.

Blue Moon over Parsippany

"*U*ncle Pete, Uncle Pete, I'm over here Uncle Pete" chirped a little voice from behind a large tree "Bet you can't find me uncle Pete" said the little voice eagerly wooing attention from her favorite uncle. Pete smiled as he recognized the little voice, "that can't be Carolyn could it?, nawhhh, Carolyn wouldn't be hiding from her uncle Pete, no sir, Carolyn would be right here hugging her favorite uncle" with that being said Carolyn dashed out from behind a tree and threw her arms around her uncle Pete. Pete reached down and with one motion swooped her tiny body up over his head. Carolyn giggled with delight "I love you Uncle Pete", "I love you too baby girl".

It wasn't often Pete would visit with family. Pete would tell his friends that he was so far removed from his family he wasn't the black sheep of the family, he's the family goat. When Pete would spend time with the family it was usually at funerals or weddings where he could make a quick exit. The only exception was to visit his younger brother Tim and his family. Tim adored his older brother and was happy to have him around. Tim, although quiet and shy, appreciated Pete's outgoing nature and gregarious spirit. Pete was the family risk taker, the entertainer, the charmer. Pete would entertain the family with his stories of fortune and fame, always swearing they were absolutely true. Pete liked Tim as well. Tim was grounded in all the family values that Pete had tossed aside many years before. Tim married his high school sweetheart, Sandy. He loved and provided for her and their 4 children. Tim was one of those people who always seemed relaxed and content with life. Tim admired Pete, and Pete admired Tim, yet neither would want to live the others life.

Sandy grew up with 4 sisters and remained close to them as an adult. Being part of a close knit family afforded Sandy and Tim's kids an assortment of cousins, aunts and uncles to grew up with. Sunday dinners and family bar-be-que 's were regular family gatherings. Tim took an immediate liking to Sandy's family. From the first time he met them Tim connected to their wholesome, traditional values. Values that Tim and Pete were not so lucky to have had as children. Growing up for them was more a matter of survival and something they didn't recollect with fond memories. Pete was happy for his brother, and the choices he made, but Pete knew it would never be a life for him; and Sandy would never have been Pete's choice of a wife. Pete recognized that his brother's wife was stayed, solid and stable. Pete found these traits admirable yet equally bothersome, especially in a mate. Pete never married, but by no means did he ever experience a scarcity for female companionship.

Pete had been looking forward to this particular visit to his brother's house. Tim and his wife Sandy lived outside of town in a small but newly constructed gated community. The Stiles brothers always had a special bond and there was seldom a holiday or birthday they did not see each other, if only briefly. Sandy loved to entertain and Tim's fiftieth birthday provided the perfect excuse to have a party. Pete was several years older than Tim but to see them together you would not know who the elder was. Both had salt and pepper hair and stout burley builds. Pete looked around the yard as he now was carrying a very contented, grinning Carolyn on his shoulder.

"Where's your daddy Carolyn?"
"Oh Uncle Pete, don't you know anything? This is a SUR-PRISE birthday party - Daddy's going to be really surprised to see you, Mommy said she didn't think you'd even come, but I knew you would" Carolyn stated definitively. "Mommy said

you wouldn't leave your bottle" giggle giggle - "Mommy's silly, you're too big for a bottle; right Uncle Pete?

Pete cleared his throat then carefully responded "hummm, you said it sweetheart, your Mommy is silly, very silly". Silently Pete seethed.

"Carolyn? How about we see what your cousins are up to" with that being said he slung her off his shoulder and onto the ground and away they went, her tiny hand engulfed in his large mitt like hand. They headed across the grass to a section of the yard where the older boys were throwing a football and the younger ones were playing tag. Carolyn broke free from her uncle's clasp and joined the group playing tag. One of the younger teenage boys tried to catch Pete off guard and threw the football in his direction but Pete surprised him as he caught it and threw it back within seconds. The group of boys were amazed at Pete's speed and agility! One older boy, who had possession of the ball, shouted to Pete, "not bad for an old man!" Pete broke into a run, catching the boy off guard by tackling him. As Pete completed the tackle, he took the ball and tossed it to a smaller boy, who was equally surprised and thrilled to finally have the ball and be part of the action. Pete casually got off the ground and nonchalantly stood over the tackled boy. Pete looked down and politely offered his hand to help the boy up while withholding any comment. The boy sheepishly took Pete's calloused hand, smiled, and acquiesced to Pete. Saying nothing the boy ran off to be with the other kids as Pete sauntered back to the deck where the adults were gathering. Sandy was busy making last minute preparations as several more guests arrived. Pete watched his sister-in-law meet and greet each guest with an obligatory hug or hand shake as she corralled them onto the deck to await the festivities. Pete, not being one to adhere to social formalities recognized several of his younger brother's friends and in his gregarious manner eagerly approached them.

"Hey, Smither, John Smither - I haven't seen you in ages! You old dog, what have you been up to?"

Smither, casually acknowledged Pete.

"Pete Stiles? I can't remember the last time I saw you either-You still live outside of town?"

Pete smiled and nodded as he shook Smither's hand and kindly slapped him on the back."Sure do -same place for the last thirty years, how about you?" Sheepishly Smither replied "I just moved back into this neighborhood, 3-weeks-ago, just a couple blocks from here;"

Momentarily surprised Pete wondered why he hadn't seen Smither before now; after all, the town wasn't that big. Dismissing the thought Pete just laughed and smiled at his old friend " How about a drink? My brother must have something with a little kick to drink around here" and with a wink and grin Pete led the way from the deck into the kitchen in his brother's house.

By this time Sandy had walked into the kitchen and was gathering trays of appetizers to take out to her guests.

"Carolyn? Carolyn where are you" Sandy cast a quick look around looking for her youngest child.   Seeing Carolyn playing, she returned to her party preparations.   Noting Pete's entrance into the kitchen with just a quick glance, Sandy was neither warm nor welcoming to Pete or John Smither- "Hello, John, surprised to see you"... as her voice trailed off he awkwardly continued - "I ran into Sam Caldwell at the hardware store last week, he told me you were having friends over for Tim's birthday and said I should stop by..." his voice trailed off. Sensing the uncomfortableness of the moment Pete interrupted the awkward silence

"The more the merrier, right Sandy?" Politely nodding she exited with her tray of appetizers. Neither Pete nor Smither was favored by Sandy but she accepted them as part of her husband's life. By now more of Tim's friends had arrived and were gathering in the kitchen having their own mini-reunion with Pete and Smither.

Pete knew where his brother might have a bottle of liquor if there was any to be found. Tim and Sandy were not big drinkers; in fact they hardly ever drank alcohol. Pete, stealthily scanning the kitchen cabinets found a bottle of Jack Daniels hidden away far out of the children's view or reach but perfect access for an adult. Cracking the bottle open, Pete poured shots for each of his brothers guests. Pete, holding his glass high leading the crew he started "Here's to Tim, wherever the SOB is," and they all broke into laughter since Tim wasn't even at the party yet. Next was Smither "To the perfect host, Tim, best damn host I've ever known..." the group broke into more laughter. Soon, more guests were in the kitchen than on the deck and Tim was due home at any moment. Carolyn came running into the kitchen, her little voice barely audible over the loud raucous laughter as she pushed through the forest of adult bodies and found her Uncle Pete. Pulling on his sleeve she desperately fought for his attention "Uncle Pete, Uncle Pete, it's time, Daddy is driving up the driveway and Mommy wants everyone on the deck to surprise him!! Come on, COME on now, we have to go NOW!!!!" Pete, enjoying the attention and the bourbon, was paying no attention to Carolyn as he proceeded to tell one more joke to his band of merry men. Carolyn frustrated with her Uncle let go of his sleeve when the screen door opened and Tim walked in. Carolyn jumped into her Daddy's arms and shouted "SURPRISE" but no one else noticed. Sandy, followed behind her husband, looked totally heartbroken. Pete, finishing one of his stories started pouring another round of shots when he noticed his brother. "Little Bro!! Big five O!! How's it going? Happy Birthday!!" and Pete gave a great big bear hug to his younger brother. Tim, a little confused, but not surprised, greeted his brother as well "Pete, can't say you ever surprise me" as he glanced at the almost empty bottle of bourbon. Gazing back at his somewhat inebriated older sibling Tim continued "You ok Pete? Let's go out on the deck and get something to eat - Looks like Sandy has been cooking all day and you know no one cooks tenderloin like Sandy" Sandy, disheartened that there was no surprise for Tim tried to resume a party attitude for her husband. Sandy enjoyed pleasing Tim and wanted the rest of the party to go well, despite her brother-in-law's disruption. When Pete started drinking anything could happen and Sandy knew enough to sit back and ride it out. Carolyn, delighted to have the attention of both her uncle and her father walked between them, holding on each of their hands. Shunned by the older kids, because of her age, Carolyn was content to be with adults. The smell of bar be que lured the guests onto the deck and the party continued. Sandy had prepared a buffet worthy of a king. Everyone enthusiastically filled their plates with assorted foods. Pete and Tim, their plates full, proceeded to sit with several other guests on the deck and engaged in small talk. Smither, who lived only a couple blocks away had left briefly with no word to anyone and returned equally unnoticed. He carried a brown paper grocery bag and sat down next to Pete. Never coy, Pete asked "What's with the bag?" Smither sheepishly responded to Pete "Thought we could use more Jack Daniels and maybe a little excitement" "Excitement? Pete thoughtfully asked as he was reaching for the Jack Daniels, Hummmm what could you have in that bag that could be considered exciting?". "Oh, you'll see" said Smither as he softly smirked before taking another swig of JD.

Focused on the Jack Daniels Pete forgot about the excitement that Smither had been speaking of. Pete loved to drink; there wasn't an event or occasion that didn't require libation. Wine was his favorite but seldom would he refuse anything else. After the initial anticipation and arrival of guests and the guest of honor (Tim), everyone settled in to eat, converse and play assorted lawn games. Pete settled in with Smither and a few select guests who were also prone to imbibe. Sandy, who efficiently set up the party, was equally efficient in cleaning up the party. Tim, schmoozed from guest to guest, always the perfect host, making sure everyone was having a good time and felt welcome. Just before dusk, Smither left Pete's band of merry men and was seen talking to Tim and Sandy. It was still too noisy to hear the conversation but Sandy could be seen shaking her head no and pleading with Tim to agree with her. Tim seemed to be reassuring Sandy that it would be alright as he clapped to get everyone's attention. Tim started to speak "Tonight we're going to have a special treat, My old friend John, er argh.. Smither, is going to set up a fireworks display for everyone to enjoy" the children shouted in delight as adults eagerly rearranged their lawn chairs for the best view. Tim continued "so sit back and enjoy – the excitement will start just after dark!" Sandy did not look thrilled but rather worried. Tim hugged her and reassured her that everything would be fine, that it would be fun. She did not look convinced.

Pete watched Smither busy himself with his bag of fireworks and booze but wasn't feeling ambitious enough to lend Smither a hand. Smither wobbled to the far side of the yard and began to set up his fireworks display. Each needed to be secured to the ground before they could be lit and Smither had a specific sequence that he wanted them set up in. Several guests had volunteered to assist in the set up but walked away as Smither became bossy and argumentative. In addition to being ornery, Smither was very drunk and appeared disinterested in this endeavor when only half the firworks were in place. He ended up setting them up all by himself in a somewhat half assed manner as he rushed to be done before dark.

The moment had come, guests were stretched out on the lawn, on blankets or lawn chairs looking toward the sky waiting for the bursts of color to be provided by Smither and his fireworks display – Smither eager to start the show, or get it over with, took the final swig of JD, tossed the empty bottle onto the lawn and with the large lighter lit all of the fuses as fast as he could, then he ran off, preparing to lite the second row before disappearing into the night.

The first set of fireworks lit up the sky with several loud popping sounds and a visual waterfall of colors. Everyone ohhhhed and awhhhhhhhhed as Smither lit the second grouping of fireworks.

Suddenly everything became chaotic.

The fireworks, which Smither had haphazardly erected, had accidentally tipped over once lit. Instead of firing up into the sky they were firing across the lawn toward the house and deck, like missiles being launched, into the unassuming crowd. In the darkness all you could see was trails of color firing across the lawn. At first the guests were confused and did not completely understand what was happening, and then they started to scream and panic as they realized they were being fired upon. Guests were grabbing their lawn chairs and using them as shields protecting themselves from the stray fireworks, each moving stealthily back to the house. Parents were frantic to find their children, couples were looking for their mates, and most were just looking for shelter. Smither, had vanished into the night. Pete, usually fixed on his feet became shaky and disoriented when he first stood up. Scrambling to find shelter he bolted across the yard, with several of the younger kids fast on his heals. Ducking behind Tim's garden shed someone started screaming from the direction of the house "the lawn's on fire quick get the hose, the lawns on fire!" The kids who where following Pete stopped following him, changed direction and were running to see the fire. Pete, gasping to catch his breath, leaned against the shed and thought he heard a child's cry. Listening closely Pete discerned Carolyn's little voice, and then a sussssh. He listened, unsure that it was her yet straining his hearing to focus on the little voice amongst the bedlam.

"I don't want to sit here anymore, I want my Mommy, I don't like it here, pleeeaaase let me go"

Pete realized the voice was coming from inside the shed, instantly, he pushed open the door and there was Carolyn sitting on drunk Smither's naked lap, his jeans down to his ankles. Seeing her Uncle Pete, Carolyn slipped free of Smither's hold and ran to the door. Pete grabbed Smither by his shirt with his left hand and hit him square in the jaw with his right fist. Not realizing that Sandy and Tim were also looking for Carolyn they heard the commotion in the shed and were seconds behind Pete as he punched Smither again. Carolyn ran out the door directly into her mother's arms as Tim ran into the shed, shocked at what he saw. Tim yelled to Sandy to take Carolyn back to the house immediately and call the police. Tim witnessed his brother's massive strength as he beat Smither with his fists, swiftly and succinctly till Smither could not get up. Just as Pete was going to level the final blow, Tim stepped in and held Pete back "He's not worth going to jail over, Sandy is calling the police, you better get out of here." Never sure what Pete's current relationship was with the police Tim thought it best Pete leave. Smither, covered in his own blood, lay motionless on the floor, his pants still down to his ankles. Tim looked at Pete and as their eyes met Tim nodded and simply said "Thank-you". Pete gave his brother a pat on the back, stepped over Smither and headed toward the door. Taking one last look at Smither Pete muttered "You no good SOB, Don't EVER cross my path or any of my family again, you got it?" Smither whimpered and groaned as Pete moved his foot closer to him, ready to launch him with one final kick. Tim moved between Pete and Smither, "You better get out of here, I'll talk to the police, just go…" Pete left the shed and was heading toward his truck when Sandy was coming out of the house, walking toward Pete. Pete started to say Sandy's name but she cut him off "Pete don't say it – just don't say anything. Why does it always have to end like this? Always chaos, always something, something terrible…"She started to cry Pete reached to comfort her but she stepped away from him as he spoke" I'm sorry, I never thought Smither was like that, honest, I never would've let anyone like that around here " Looking directly at Pete, Sandy spoke in very calming tones, tears still streaming down her face "I know Pete, You may not be directly responsible, you never are, but somehow things happen, crazy, out of control, bad things, when you are around…" Sandy stopped speaking as a police car pulled into the driveway, its lights flashing as an ambulance also pulled in close behind. Looking to Sandy for direction Pete asked if he should stay. Sandy, looking baffled and somewhat amused at his question replied politely "No Pete, its ok, the police and ambulance will be able to handle it". Looking relived to leave, Pete flashed a nervous grin at his sister-in law, as he climbed awkwardly into his truck and drove off into the night.

"Most people never run far enough on their first wind to find out they have a second"

—William James

Liam's Life

"**I** don't understand what all the fuss is about. I drank a couple beers, and smoked a little weed, that's it. Now probation rules my life – where I go, who I see. I'm talking to a counselor and going to AA. All I want to do is chill. Everyone else is doing the same things I've done yet I'm the one who got caught. Really, it's no big deal."

For as long as he could remember all Liam wanted to do was play in a band.

"My life story is about music. Music has always been the center of my life. My parents met while my Dad was hitchhiking across the country following the Grateful Dead. My Mom was his ride between Phoenix and San Francisco and I was conceived somewhere between there and Denver. Mom played the guitar and Dad played the radio. Until I was old enough to begin school the only home I knew was the backseat of a Ford Fairlaine. We'd travel from town to town, Dad working odd jobs and Mom singing in coffee houses or roadside taverns. When I was old enough for kindergarten, we moved in with my grandmother (mom's mom). Everything changed. Now I had lunch times and bed times; school clothes and play clothes; Dad went

46

to work with my Grandpa at a local garage. Mom stayed at home. We seemed "normal". This worked for a couple years until my grandmother died and then it changed again".

Liam's grandmother died when he was 10-years-old. The regularity and predictability of day to day living that he had come to know, ended. Liam's grandmother not only cared for the family but she always made Liam feel special. She would talk and really listen to him when no one else had time. She taught Liam to read music and play the piano. Liam's dad continued working at the garage with grandpa but Liam couldn't count on him to be home at any special time. And when dad got home, Mom was out the door. Liam's mom was home alone during the day and she jumped at the opportunity to leave every evening to sing at a local tavern. "I can't remember the three of us being together after Grandma died. We each did our own thing. I went to school (or not) depending on whether I woke up in time or felt like going. No one really paid attention to me." "I missed being a family and would try to spend time with my Dad and grandpa at the garage when school got out – but I felt as if I was in the way and not really welcomed. I wasn't mechanically inclined and felt out of place. I was way more comfortable at the tavern waiting for mom to sing. The waitresses, bartenders and other performers became the family I wanted." Bartenders got use to seeing Liam and treated him like an adult, even letting him have an occasional glass of beer. They would feed him and entertain him, and made him feel special.

"Like your grandmother did?" I asked Liam

"What? Made me feel special? I guess so" his voice trailed off as if thinking about another time or place. I encouraged him to continue; Liam hesitated then resumed his story

"Waitresses would share secrets with me and confine in me like I was a brother. I liked hearing tavern gossip and tales of heart break and romantic mystery. Other times, I would shoot pool or play pin ball until it was time for my mom to sing. I always loved to hear her sing. In between sets she would show me a cord or two on her guitar and I would sing along – making my own harmonies. Life was perfect".

By the time Liam was 15-years –old he dropped out of school. He was the dishwasher at the bar by day and back up singer for my Mom at night. Soon he was singing with other performers and was busy almost every night. When he turned 17-yrs-old he recalled "I gave up my "day job" washing dishes. I thought I'd made it big! I had hooked up with a band and was singing every night. Sure, some of the places we were playing in were dives, but we wanted the exposure (and the free beer wasn't a bad perk)."

Traveling from town to town was tiring and Liam started to use crank to stay awake. "I'd snort a couple lines of crank to get me going and swallow a couple bennys to go to sleep. Somehow my days and nights blended together just like the bars and towns we traveled thru. I couldn't hear the music I couldn't see the sights. My world was a big blurrr." Liam paused, looked to see if I was attentive before he continued "Then one night changed everything." "We were playing a gig in a small town in south west Kentucky, I had been shit-faced for days - but we needed cash and the bar needed a band. I knew I wasn't in any condition to play but there were no other prospects for work. The van needed gas and we needed beer. As show time approached I had a harder time than usual waking up- ha! Waking up, standing up, neither seemed likely! I was totally wasted! The other guys weren't in much better shape but somehow they got me on my feet and pointed me toward the stage. I teetered cautiously onto the stage, blinded by the lights I raised my arm to shield my eyes, still moving forward robotically moving into position to perform. Suddenly I became afraid, I thought someone was after me and the room was so noisy I couldn't hear or see the rest of the band. I panicked and bolted blindly forward and with one grand leap I soared off the stage and into the crowd. Crazy as it sounds the crowd thought it was cool and started chanting" JUMP! JUMP! JUMP! taunting the other band members to also jump. The band was still toasted and didn't hesitate to follow my lead and each one, jumped into the crowd. Someone (probably the guy we landed on) was very drunk and very angry and landed a right hook to the side of my head. Hell broke loose. Fists were flying, bottles were braking. Total chaos, as I desperately fought my way toward the exit, still convinced someone was after me. Just as I reached my destination someone put a hand on the back of my neck, holding me from leaving"

A deep, loud voice said "You're not going anywhere"

"No, just watch me" and I bolted free from his grip and I swung around hitting him square in the jaw- impressed with the accuracy of the blow and the pain in my hand, I hesitated to run

"Now you did it, you are under arrest...." as he tackled me to the ground, flipped me onto my belly and cuffed my hands behind my back I heard him read me my rights but it made little difference, I knew I was screwed."

"60 days in jail, a shit load of fines and enough restitution that I could own the dive, and I'm still stuck in Kentucky. I'll do whatever to get out of here so I'm washing dishes to my pay fines; talking to counselors and on probation. "Hey, what's the fuss? I drank a couple beers, and smoked a little weed..

"The Moth don't care when he sees The Flame.
He might get burned, but he's in the game.
And once he's in, he can't go back, he'll
Beat his wings 'til he burns them black...
No, The Moth don't care when he sees The Flame. . .
The Moth don't care if The Flame is real,
'Cause Flame and Moth got a sweetheart deal.
And nothing fuels a good flirtation,
Like Need and Anger and Desperation...
No, The Moth don't care if The Flame is real. . . "

—Aimee Mann

Baffled, Bewildered and Bemused

I was born and raised in Bergen County, New Jersey, a suburb of NYC. I guess you could call me a "baby boomer", born in the 1950's and becoming a teenager in the 1960s. A relatively large numbers of my peers also became teenagers during this time. We were too young to have any personal memory of World War II, but old enough to benefit from the postwar American high. To say Boomers grew up at a time of dramatic social change was an understatement. In the United States, whether it was politics (Vietnam war), religion (traditional v. contemporary), music (rock and roll), social morals (sexual freedom), civil rights, or the advent of transistor radios and television, as a society, we were changing rapidly. These social changes set the stage for generational conflicts caused by strong cultural differences between the younger, idealistic proponents of social change and the more conservative, traditional "old guard".

I grew up in a neighborhood that was predominantly Irish Catholic, working class. It was me, my three brothers and my parents. My Mom was a stay at home mother, just like the other moms in our neighborhood. As we grew up she worked part time at a local stationary store, more for something to keep her busy than the money. Dad commuted into NYC daily just as many of our neighbor's dads did. In the mornings you would see the fathers walking to the bus stops, wearing their suits and carrying briefcases, waiting to depart for NYC. At the end of the day they would return, getting off the bus and walking back home. Just like clockwork their arrival was predictable. On weekends, Dad was a baseball coach and scoutmaster. My brothers and I each went to school, church and cub scouts. We played little league baseball. We helped at potluck suppers and volunteered at hospital candy sales. We were close in age, even called Irish twins since two of my brothers were born in the same year. My brothers, Donavan and Frank were the oldest, then me, and then the youngest, Patrick; were my best friends and their friends were my friends.

Everyone in our neighborhood knew each other and belonged to the same parish. We were alter boys on Sundays, hell-raisers Monday thru Saturday. I had a wonderful childhood, mom dad and three brothers– we were not rich but we were happy. I don't remember wanting for anything. Life was good.

Not far from our neighborhood was an area known as the swamps. Some of my fondest childhood memories are of summer days spent playing there. We would get up early, pack a lunch, rally our friends and ride our bikes out of town, toward the highway and behind the industrial area to the swamps – Now it's the Meadowlands, home of the N.J. Giants football team.

The swamps seemed to be a supernatural play place where we seem stronger, smarter, more daring and more courageous than we were in "the real world". We could ride dirt bikes, burn cat-tails (punks) and smoke cigarettes. We were the lords of the land - we were in charge and we made the rules - no adults! And we were free!

As we grew up the swamps were less for make-believe and more for making-out. We smoked Marijuana, drank beer and boasted of our triumphs with girls. In the wake of the Vietnam War, all of the above activities were acceptable pastimes, almost a customary right of passage into adulthood. Some of us made this transition with grace and dignity. Others, like me, chose the less polished, awkward shift toward manhood.

I was a gear-head as far back as I can remember. I loved to take things apart and put them back together again. Alarm clocks, transistor radios, and lawn mowers, you name it. I could sit for hours "tinkering". Being able to fix things gave me a sense of personal contentment because I was accomplishing and achieving something.

I was the neighborhood kid who could fix your bike, change a tire, or rebuild your engine. Once I was in High School all I really wanted was a car – and my life focus became getting one. I stopped playing sports and I started working odd jobs – I did whatever it took to make some cash, and the more the better. I hung around neighborhood garages and junk yards waiting for the chance to make a couple dollars. Mostly I ran their errands, sometimes to the parts store, or junk yard, but mostly to the liquor store. Beer and Brandy were the favorites. Clerks rarely questioned my age and if they did, I would tell them who had sent me – I always got served. But money was slow coming and I was impatient. So I took the money I had saved and "invested" in marijuana. The turn around time was fast and the profit was high with little effort. I soon became quite the entre-preneur, investing in an assortment of products (drugs) in an effort to meet my customer's demands. I didn't want to involve my brothers so I stayed away from them. I spent more time on the street than I did at home.

Even though I wasn't using drugs they became my life. The money I was making selling drugs became my God and I was as addicted to the money as any addict was to the drugs. Money dominated my thoughts, dreams and plans. Everything I did revolved around when, where, and how I would get more cash. Working on cars no longer interested me. Sure I could buy cars, nice cars, but they were just transportation. I no longer cared about the satisfaction I use to get in making it work or being able to fix it. I was too busy, 24/7.

As time went by, so did my appreciation for simple things. I stopped laughing because everything seemed serious. I stopped trusting because I thought everyone was trying to rip me off. I stopped having fun because I had to be cool. I was never vulnerable, never yielding, always defensive, always on guard. I carried a gun. I was never really happy, and always really alone. My younger brother Patrick idolized me and wanted to hang out with me but I just shunned him and ordered him away. I was too cool for kids.

One fall evening while I was walking home with a pound of "new product" purchased from a supplier, who wasn't well-known to me, I sensed I was being followed. I quickened my pace as the steps behind me became quicker. I cut through a park but the shadowy character was still behind me. I was breathing heavy and my heart was pounding. I broke into a run and dodged down a familiar ally, thru a yard and then I detoured into a church, whose doors, I knew, were always unlocked. Successfully eluding my pursuer, I sat in a pew and caught my breath. No one else was in the church but me. It was at that moment that I felt a sense of peace that I had not had in a long time. I felt safe. I had not been to mass in many years yet the comfort and security I felt at that moment in that church reminded me of my childhood. I stayed still and quiet for what felt like hours but in reality was only a couple minutes. Believing that it would be safe to leave, I furtively left the pew, made the sign of the cross and left the church. As I went through the big oak door I looked both ways and came face to face with two, familiar local bullies. They were brothers named Sean and James, brothers I knew growing up. Sean was my age and James was a year or two younger. Both were known to sell drugs in the same neighborhood where I lived. Neither was known for their brains. Sean grabbed my arm as James hit me in the face, I dropped to my knees as Sean lost his grip on my arm. I rolled and jumped to my feet as James hit me again, knocking me to the ground. Within seconds Sean was on top of me hitting me in the face while James was kicking my sides, I felt as if I was going to pass out so I reached into my pocket and pulled out my gun - blood was streaming into my eyes so I couldn't see and without aiming I fired one shot. I heard James, who had been kicking me, gasp and fall over me - while Sean was already on his feet, screaming at me "YOU BASTARD, YOU SHOT MY BROTHER, YOU SHOT MY BROTHER, James? JAMES? ANSWER ME!!!!! James was laying face down, as I pulled my legs out from under him and crawled away from the bleeding corpse. Soon people were every where; medics appeared and were trying to resuscitate James. Sean was screaming and shouting and crying. Everyone was looking at me, my blood, from being beat up and James blood, from being shot, Sean covered in sweat and tears. Un-enounced to me I was still clutching my gun, the gun that killed James. The police kindly approached me and asked if I fired the gun, I nodded; they took my gun, read me my rights, put me in cuffs and gently escorted me to jail. I said nothing, resigned to the consequences of this event.

I sat in jail until my trial. My family did not visit me or accept my phone calls. None of my street friends acknowledged me. At first I wanted to plead guilty and not even have a trial but my lawyer convinced me that although I pulled the trigger my intention was not to kill anyone. My public defender tried to justify self defense but the general rule is that a homicide is neither murder nor manslaughter if it is justified or excused, as would be in the case of self defense. However, killing someone is not self defense, especially since I had the only gun.

Although my intention was not to kill James, he died as a result of my action. The fact is that none of this would have happened if I wasn't buying and selling drugs. I was charged and convicted of second degree reckless manslaughter, intent to distribute a controlled substance, and possession of a controlled substance. I served 8 years of a 5-10 sentence with a 2 year State parole tail and 5 years probation. My years in jail went slowly, every day the same, just passing time. When I was released after 8 years incarceration the door swung open and I walked out, a black plastic garbage bag with all my possessions held in one hand. My younger brother, Patrick, had agreed to let me stay with him until I got on my feet but no one else showed any interest in me.

It wasn't too long after I was released from prison, I recalled that scary autumn night and I returned to the church where I had sought refuge. It was a scene I had played over and over in my head, many times while I was in prison. I thought about how quickly the whole evening went wrong, and what I would've done differently. I was eager to visit the church where I hid out so many years ago, where my life changed forever. I entered that same church through the same door I had sought refuge in many years before. I hadn't been to confession since I was a kid and I felt as if it would be the right thing to do. Even though I knew the ritual I felt awkward going through the familiar motions. I knew it was something I needed to do.

"Father, please forgive me for I have sinned...." I confessed everything - the drugs, the shooting, how I disappointed my parents and alienated my brothers. I left the confessional heading toward the exit, unaware that anyone else was there. I was deep in my thoughts, hoping I didn't forget anything, hoping I was forgiven. As I was leaving, a priest met me at the door. He caught me off guard with his easy manner and friendly approach. He introduced himself as "Ian, Father Ian". We started talking and it was as if we had always known each other. Father Ian told me he remembered me from my childhood neighborhood; he lived on the next street over and was several years older than me. I did not remember him. We laughed about an old moped that my younger brother, Patrick, had sold to his younger sister and how it would stall out every time it got hot, often leaving the rider stranded. He remembered riding dirt bikes and playing in the swamps, just as I did. We both acknowledged a lot had changed since those days of seemingly innocence. I sheepishly told him about my time in prison and about selling drugs. I admitted to loosing track of family and old friends once I got involved with drugs. He understood completely and shared about his own battle with addiction. Just as his addiction was to alcohol, mine was to money. He talked about life being unmanageable, feeling empty and out of control, everything focusing on the next drink. I understood. My life focused on the next deal, the next sale, making money. Several hours later, as I left the church and said my good bye to father Ian, he offered me his hand and we shook, and then embraced. I felt oddly at peace and content to have a new friend.

That evening, I told my brother about the encounter with the priest. Patrick listened intently as I told him how at ease and kind the priest was. "It felt so good to talk to someone and not feel like I was being judged" I felt as if I might finally be able to forgive myself for James death, and for all the needless pain I caused my family. Patrick asked "which priest?" and I said "Father Ian", Patrick's expression changed, quickly becoming morose and his voice became very quiet, as if to share a secret, he asked if I knew that Father Ian was Sean and James older brother. Ian was the oldest brother, the one who left home and the neighborhood several years before I would've known him. I felt the color wash out of my face as I realized that Ian was the older brother of James, whom I killed. I felt light headed as my mind raced through this days events and this new piece of information. I felt confused and unable to understand the kindness extended to me by this gentle man. Patrick said no one knew where Ian had gone after he finished High School. He didn't keep in touch with anyone, even his family were unsure of where he went so they stopped talking about him. Not long after I was arrested, Ian returned to the neighborhood, assigned as the new priest to the local perishes. His family didn't know what to make of this career choice since Ian had not had "the calling" when he lived at home. No one knew what had happened to Ian in the years between leaving home and returning as a priest and no one felt comfortable asking. They were just happy to have him back, especially after what happened to James. Father Ian was known for being steadfast in his beliefs and unwavering in his faith. And that was enough for his family and parishioners.

It took me awhile to process everything that happened. I went to Sunday mass and occasionally saw Father Ian; we would nod and smile at each other but never conversed the way we did when we first met. It's as if we said it all that one time and there really was nothing left to say. With time, I was able to regain balance to my life. It wasn't easy, I no longer needed immediate gratification from fast money. And I no longer chose to profit from the misfortune of others. I work a regular job and make regular money. My life isn't perfect but its progress not perfection. I will always be prone to excess but by staying vigilant and alert to my defects of character I won't repeat the past.

"People don't recognize that prescription drugs can kill you," "They don't recognize that prescription drugs are highly addictive. They often think they're safe because after all it's just a prescription."

—Gil Kerlikowske, the Obama Administration White House 'drug czar,'
(Join Together , Feb.24, 2011)

Crossing Mariposa Skies

Iris was raised in a good Christian home with good hard working parents. She had siblings who were as mischievous as she, but were never considered bad. They were never in any major trouble and in many respects seemed ordinary. Everyone in their family went to church weekly and school daily. She grew up, finished school and got married to a good hard -working man, Joe. Iris never had any ambitions beyond having a husband, children, and a home of her own. Her life was predictable and safe. Iris was very happy to raise her children and take care of her home. Iris belonged to the PTA and the community women's club. Her life was very simple, never frenzied, and Iris liked it that way.

Iris' children, Nicki and Jody, were still in elementary school, when Iris was driving to pick them up from an after school activity. As Iris neared the school she slowed down and began to scan the groups of bobbing heads playing in the playground, hoping to see Nicki and Jody. Caught off guard, a ball rolled out in front of her car. Iris reacted immediately by rapidly hitting her brakes. The brakes locked and screeched as Iris tried desperately to stop the car it continued to move uncontrollably forward. From behind Iris heard the sound of more screeching brakes and car horns - without any plan she instinctively braced herself knowing the car behind her would surely plow into her. The car behind was moving with such force it crunched the side door panels forward, lodging the doors shut of Iris' car. The impact threw Iris over the steering wheel and into the dashboard. Her small frame was tossed like a rag doll aimlessly landing wherever thrown. She was not wearing a safety belt. Iris' knees were wedged into the dashboard, blood was streaming down her face from a gash in her head, her arms were pinned under the console making it impossible to move. Violently, another car gave the final crash and pushed Iris' car into a telephone pole. Mercifully, she passed out from the pain.

Two days later, Iris woke up in Norfolk General Hospital. Two broken ribs, an injured spleen, a broken arm, a broken femur, a dislocated knee, three-fractured vertebrae in her neck, and too many stitches to count. It hurt to breath. She was stitched and casted from head to toe. The pain was so excruciatingly bad that she wanted to die. Her doctors were able to manipulate her arm and hand in such as way that Iris could self medicate herself by reaching the morphine pump. Iris grinned sheepishly as she recalled the relief she obtained from the morphine. When the pain became noticeable, she would press the pump and a predefined amount of morphine was injected into her IV. Sometimes she would press the pump fearful that without morphine the pain would return. This was fine for the first week or two until they decided it was time to start making Iris move around and try to walk. Once again, the pain became so bad that she was paralyzed by the discomfort. Iris winced as she recalled the pain "I asked for morphine and the doctors denied me it" I was told to "push past the pain". "I could not." I was furious that my pain was not being treated" Iris remembered refusing to walk or leave her bed stating the pain was intolerable." Iris's family and friends urged her to cooperate but Iris insisted that the pain was unbearable - "the longer I go between injections, the worse I feel" she pleaded. "I get chills right to my bones, my muscles ache and I feel nauseous". Eventually, she was injected regularly with Demerol or Dilaudid for the pain. Between injections she was given Vicodin or Percocets, which she swallowed like candy. After a month and a half Iris was allowed to go home. As Iris was awaiting discharge a hospital employee, whom she did not recognize came to her room. "Hi, are you Iris? My name is Silvia Hendricks; I'm a psychiatric /addictions nurse specialist. The hospital requires that I talk to every client who has had long term trauma treatment or who will be using prescribed narcotics to have an exit interview with me, is that ok with you?' hesitantly Iris agreed, uncomfortable with the casual manner Ms. Hendricks presented. Iris thought "this is a waste of time". After several routine administrative questions Nurse Hendricks pointedly asked Iris "Have you ever decided to stop drinking/drugging for a week or so, but only lasted for a couple of days?" Iris was shocked, "What??? EXCUSE ME? I thought this was about trauma and my medication - NOT alcohol!! I'm not an alcoholic. From the first time I tasted liquor it did not appeal to me. I never felt any pressure to drink nor did I have friends who drank. It just wasn't part of my life. "Iris' voice became louder and she became more offended as Nurse Hendricks tried to explain the reason for her questions but Iris was not having any of it.

"Drugs are a foreign concept to me. I do not take them lightly and I could not imagine smoking or drinking anything recreationally. I take medication which helps with my pain! All my medications are Dr. prescribed and purchased at a pharmacy. I have complete control of myself and the medications I take. What kind of person do you think I am! One thing for sure, I Am Not an addict." And with that Nurse Hendricks left several brochures on Iris' nightstand, wished her well and left her room. Iris was ready to leave, with the aid of a walker, her husband and a Percocet (or two) she was homeward bound! Casting a last glance around the room Iris saw the brochures and didn't bother to even look at them. Iris thought the worst was over, boy was she wrong!

Iris was thrilled to go home. Joe and the children wel-comed her back and tried to make everything perfect. Nicki and Jody decorated a banner and hung it over the door; Joe bought Iris' favorite foods, even though she ate very little. Iris still had pain and needed to use a walker but other than that she said she felt fine. Well, almost fine. She would move or sit in a par-ticular way and the pain would shoot thru her body. "I felt as if it would never stop." Iris crossed her hands on her lap and anx-iously tapped her foot, as if even the memory could cause her distress "Sometimes I would actually thrash back and forth from the pain." "I felt like the pain would never end yet in real-ity it probably only lasted a couple minutes or so." I would desperately maneuver myself to wherever my Percocet's were and I would swallow two or three as fast as possible. I could swallow them without any water when the pain was so bad. But, I would wait, patiently for the medicine to kick in. Slowly, I could feel my body relax as if the pain was being washed away by the tide of Percocet's. I could breath normally – the pain was gone. I thought everything was perfect again", for the moment. Iris' family noticed the difference in her disposition but found ways to blame her nastiness on everything she had been through. Joe felt guilty for getting impatient with Iris' moods because he thought he was just fortunate she was alive. Iris could be nice and gracious to her family as long as she felt no pain. The pain tested her patience and tolerance for the smallest things. She could not be bothered with details.

Months after her hospital discharge Iris claimed no improvement, although the doctors were pleased with her physical progress. There were no physical indications support-ing Iris' claim of pain. Upon hearing this Iris demanded sec-ond and third opinions. "Everything seemed to impose on my life. No one seemed to realize that as long as I had my pills everything was fine. I just needed my pain pills. Soon Iris became fearful of feeling pain and she could predict when the pills would wear off, so in anticipation of the pain she would take a Percocet as a precaution.

Her days consisted of a pill or two before getting out of bed, a pill with coffee, another pill or two mid morning, 2 more afternoon and mid afternoon, 2 after supper and 2 to go to bed. Any where between 10 and 12 pills guaranteed a pain free day. At first her family seemed pleased that Iris was not in pain but soon they became demanding of what they expected of her. They wanted the Iris they knew and loved before the accident. Iris chuckles as she cites life after the accident but on pain killers - For instance, She no longer felt it to be important to sweep or vacuum the floor daily, dirty dishes could sit in the sink and laundry could be done once a week. She found herself feeling so restful that she could nap several times a day sometimes even nodding out in mid-sentence. Iris had convinced herself that the peacefulness that she was experiencing now was far better than the rocketing pain that she had experienced before. Although she had not experienced pain in several months she knew that the pain was there and if she stopped taking my pills, it would be worse than ever. She was not going to chance it.

More months had gone by since Iris had been discharged from the hospital - Iris was at a routine follow-up visit when she complained to her surgeon that the Percocet's were no longer working and that she needed something stronger – he gave her a prescription for Oxycodin, with instructions to only take them when needed for pain. She agreed. Iris raced to the pharmacy, filled the prescription and took two while still in the parking lot. Unsure of how they would work and fearful that the pain would return she took one more for good measure. The third was not a charm – She became light headed and so so very relaxed. Iris did not remember driving home or getting into her bed. Iris began to cry, "I woke up 1 day later, still in my street clothes, my husband and children next to the bed saying how frightened they were that I didn't wake up". "Joe said the car had several new large dents on the passenger side and I could care less. The fear in Jody and Nicki's eyes meant nothing to me, after all no one understood my pain, and Joe seemed more concerned about the car than me! " Two days after that, the pain was once again, unbearable. Iris took two Oxycodin, maybe two more and possibly two other pills that she thought were antacids. Quietly resting, Iris' family did not notice and were grateful that she was sleeping peacefully. They were so use to her sleeping they didn't think anything of it till a whole day had passed and she had not come out of her room. Finally, Jody went in to show his mom a 100 he received on a spelling test. When she did not wake or move he panicked, fearful his mom was dead. Immediate calls were placed to 911, and Iris was whisked off to the hospital in an ambulance; her pulse was faint and her breathing shallow. This was the first of what was soon to become a somewhat often occurrence. Overdosing, trips to the hospital, stomach pumping and back home. An endless cycle.

Iris had become her own doctor – She no longer trusted anyone to medicate her, after all who knew her pain better than her? She knew what to take when she woke up and what to take throughout the day and throughout the night. Awkwardly Iris admitted that "Sometimes when I needed more pills I'd confused one pill with another and I'd end up at the hospital; that's how I'd overdose" Once again Joe stayed by her side; her children stricken with fear. Iris would wake up, get sent home and the cycle would start all over again. "My days and nights blended into one. My life was an endless succession of infomercials, celebrity game shows and reality TV." Rebounding from her moment of remorse Iris flew into instant justification stating "Don't think this was an easy life, I had plenty of stress. Doctor's would stop writing me scripts; pharmacies would question my use. Some doctors had the nerve to suggest physical therapy; others suggested holistic pain management." Realizing the potential to be "cut off" from her medication, Iris started hording pills. "My life centered on the pills". Pondering her last statement, Iris closed her eyes and in a whisper said "funny, somewhere amongst the chaos, I forgot about the pain, or maybe it no longer existed, I just wanted my pills"

Doctors became less sympathetic toward Iris' cries of pain and started to ignore her requests for pain medication. Iris started traveling further from home to different doctors and Iris learned how to "Dr. shop", Iris would look for doctors who were known to charge more but give YOU what YOU needed. Iris' stockpile of prescription pain killers drugs grew. Still being fearful of running out, and still using 20 plus pills a day, Iris would go into the medicine cabinets of family and friends, looking for and taking drugs of interest. "The only time I felt well enough to leave my sofa or bed, was when I needed more pills". "Days turned to weeks and weeks turned to months." With her stash getting low and fewer doctors giving her prescriptions Iris was tiring of the cycle of doctors, prescriptions, and pills. She decided to take a short cut and steal a prescription pad from a somewhat careless, yet trusting, doctor. Feeling over confident and guilt free, Iris had new ambition to – write and fill prescriptions. She justified this illegal act by remembering the pain from her accident, the insensitivity of her doctors and the inconvenience of finding new doctors and having to convince them of the degree of pain, she felt. Iris knew what she needed and could further justified her actions smugly she would say, "I was paying for my prescription, I had insurance. It wasn't like I was taking the doctors time away from other sick people, I was freeing up their time by writing my own scripts".

Believing she was very talented as well as efficient Iris was managing just fine until a new pharmacist started questioning the dose, necessity and regularity of her prescriptions. Her life fell apart quickly. With both children watching, Iris was arrested for prescription fraud, hand cuffed, and taken to jail. Iris was humiliated tremendously. She was "processed" (finger printed, photographed and strip-searched) at the county prison before having a bail hearing. Her husband dutifully posted her bail and took Iris home, never saying a word. There was nothing either one could say. The shame and guilt were more than Iris could stand. The worst part was not having her husband Joe's support. "The silence was enough to kill me"

Iris cried and continued through clenched teeth "That night, when I got home, I swallowed my stash. I really wanted to die. Instead of dying, little did I know I would get my life back, 100 times better than I ever dreamed."

Iris woke up in intensive care, with no family present. She asked for her husband and children but they were nowhere to be seen. They stayed at home and would only call and speak to staff regarding her condition; they would not speak to her. Iris begged for their attention and howled for medicine. Iris received neither. For 7 days, Iris physically detoxed from prescription drugs. Her perceived pain was unbearable. Iris would sweat and then have chills, nausea, diarrhea and head ache; a million times worse than any flu she'd ever had. She would be wide awake, and unable to sleep. Iris did not believe it would ever end. However, it did. Slowly, and gradually Iris was able to eat and sleep.

Finally, her doctor, her husband Joe, both children, and Nurse Hendricks came to see her. No flowers, no tears; just an ultimatum. Either Iris gets help or goes directly to jail. Criminal charges were still pending and the county was willing to accept a deal of rehab instead of jail and 2-year probation to follow. Iris smirked as she recalled her reaction "Not going to jail sounded great, but REHAB – ME? NO WAY! I am not an addict; I used prescription drugs, not street drugs. I kept reciting over and over "I'm NOT an Addict, I'm NOT an addict, but no one listened." Iris ordered everyone out of her room and finally, they after everyone had left and Iris was feeling somewhat secure in her apparent victory over jail and rehab, a stout, cheery faced, women asked if she could visit with her. Seeing no harm or threat, Iris agreed. This woman sat by her bed, held her hand, and told Iris the most incredible story of a woman addicted to prescription drugs, who lost her family, home and job because of her addiction. Tears filled Iris' eyes "At first I didn't want to listen but the more she spoke, the more mesmerized I was by her story. I was too tired to fight, too tired to defend my drugs. Her story was my story. She's an addict and I'm an addict. Somehow in my emotional haze she made sense. I agreed to go to rehab".

Iris was admitted to a long-term rehab. Iris learned how to manage her pain without narcotics and how to live without pills. Each day became easier as Iris accepted her addiction as a part of her, not all of her. Iris realized that the disease of addiction, which she has, may be dormant at this moment but could become active. Drugs or alcohol, she's vulnerable to both. It took time, and family therapy, but Iris was able to restore her relationship with her Joe and her children. Her priorities and choices are clear, not tainted by a drug-induced fog. Iris smiled "I know with every fiber of my being that I am and always will be a drug addict; a drug addict in recovery".

When the world says, "Give up,"
Hope whispers, "Try it one more time."
—Author Unknown

The Runner and the Race

Gloria entered my office and sat directly across from me. She plopped into an over stuffed arm chair that seemed to engulf her small frame, throwing one leg over the arm rest. Her arms crossed defiantly across her chest, her eyes locked onto mine, challenging me to start this session. She had repeatedly stated she had nothing to say yet for some reason unenounced to me; today she was ready to talk. For over a year, once a week she would be here for her appointment, and almost ritualistically she would say she had nothing to say. Gloria was required by social services to meet with a therapist once a week if she was to keep her daughter. Defiantly, she would remind me that social services could make her attend but they could not make her talk. So every week we went through this drill. Yet today was different. Almost as if inviting me to disagree with her she started "My childhood sucked. My mother was a whore and my father a drunk. Everyone I knew drank or drugged. I try not to think about my childhood because I become angry. After all, I'm a grown woman with a kid of my own – I don't need to think about the past." She was right, her past was a nightmare.

Gloria's chart held essential administrative information. Gloria was the third child of four. There were other children but

67

the four that Gloria grew up with had the same mom and dad. Speaking in a fast, monotone voice Gloria continued "My brothers were older and my sister was the baby. My mom wasn't ever really a part of my life." All us kids were close in age, all being 9 -12 months apart – as were the rest of her children. Gloria's mom was good at having kids but not interested in raising kids. She left when Gloria was 2 years old and never returned. Gloria continued "I remember crying myself to sleep, wondering where my mom was and why she left us with HIM. I was so envious of kids who had both parents and at least one good parent who loved them. I had neither. My father was no prize. He seemed extra angry after she left almost as if he blamed us for his miserable life. We learned real early to take care of each other and to stay out of his way. He thought nothing of back handing us across the face or beating us with whatever was in reach. I was terrified of HIM. He always smelt of alcohol and diesel fuel." "My father was a mechanic at a local garage and didn't take a lot of pride in his appearance. He boasted of how he never missed a day of work and raised his four kids without anyone's help. He was gruff and mean – only meaner after a day of work and a case of beer. We were terribly afraid of him. As my brothers grew up they would try to stand up to him only to be beaten within an inch of their lives. They left home as soon as they were able. I wanted so badly for HIM to care about me that I tried to please HIM by acting "grown up"." She stopped and looked at me, needing encouragement to continue. I asked her" to tell me more". At 11 years old I was cooking meals, doing the laundry, and caring for my younger sister. Most of the time my dad didn't even notice. Until one day, my father came home really drunk and really angry. He tripped as he came into the room and looked directly at me, as if I had something to do with him tripping. His expression changed from rage to a smirk as he commented on how much I looked like my mother – he moved closer to me and I could smell his foul body odor and the stale smoke and beer on his breath, - I froze in place. He grabbed my arm and ordered me to come with him. It was then that the nightmare really began. From that day on, whenever my father became drunk and angry he would grab me and make me go with him – alone". Gloria whimpered but took a deep breath and continued in the same fast paced mono toned voice, "My father was never kind or gentle but almost hateful in the way he touched me. At first I would cry but that only made him angrier and then he would order me to shut up, or if he was really mad he'd hit me. He'd force himself on me, sometimes making me bleed always making me feel dirty. He would talk about my mother being a slut and then remind me that I looked like her, and acted like her. And then rape me. The first time Gloria ran away from home she was 12 – she had had enough, enough cooking and cleaning and school and HIM. She just wanted to get away from it all. So one night Gloria pretended to be asleep after she was sure her father had passed out from drinking. Gloria could hear him snoring, and she knew this was her chance. HE had fallen asleep in his lounge chair near the front door so Gloria went into the bathroom and escaped through the window. She slide off the roof and landed on the ground and as fast as she could she ran into the night - away from HIM. She ran as fast and as far as she could never looking back knowing if he caught up with her he'd beat her senseless. "I didn't trust anyone and I feared having to go back to my father's house. I figured I would just leave town – other than that I had no plan". Gloria stopped talking as if to collect her thoughts, then she continued.

"I walked and walked till I finally walked to the edge of town. It had begun to rain and I could feel the water running down my face and neck – chilling me as I walked even faster. A car pulled up along side me and rolled down the window asking if I needed a ride. I saw it was a police car and I thought" this is perfect! I'm finally safe" I climbed in and thought everything would be fine, I remember thinking over and over "I'm safe, I'm really safe." The police officer took Gloria back to his headquarters, gave her a cup of hot cocoa and reassured her everything would be fine. Gloria told him everything, about the abuse and her father. Wistfully Gloria sneered "I thought he was listening. He LOOKED like he was listening, but he could not have heard a word because when I was done he told me to get my coat on cause he was taking me home." Gloria recalled her jaw dropping as she couldn't believe her ears – "Home? To MY home? What about MY Father??" At that point she started to cry realizing that this police officer was serious. He was taking her back to her father's house and there was nothing she could do. "I remember crying and pleading but it didn't matter". The police officer said "it was too late at night to find a foster home and chances are this would all be forgotten in the morning – after all, kids fight with their parents all the time – probably just a disagreement that got blown out of proportion". Gloria looked at me, tears streaming down her face, the memory being as painful as a fresh wound as she stated "I knew the worst was yet to come".

Gloria recalled the ride home in the patrol car as being silent. As the patrol car pulled up to her Father's house the front light turned on and she could see the silhouette of her father's massive frame outlined by the doorway. The police office walked Gloria to the door, told her Father he found her walking the streets and thought to return her. Gloria's Father thanked him and she was returned, like a runaway dog, to the master. The door closed, separating Gloria and her Father from the safety and security of the police officer. "It was just me and HIM. Apparently woke out of a sound sleep and not really sure of what just happened, gave me a slight advantage." HE stumbled back to his chair, too drunk to remember, to drunk to care. "The last sound I remembered hearing was his slurred speech ordering me to go to bed". "I scampered off realizing I was out of harm's way for the time being!"

Gently encouraged to go on with her story, Gloria declared that once returned home she immediately started planning her next escape. "Somewhere deep inside I knew there had to be something better in the world for me". "This couldn't be all there is to life". Even though Gloria never experienced anything better she seemed to know instinctively that there was something better out there. "Just like in the dead of winter, when everything is cold, barren and frozen in time deep down inside

70

you always know that it won't last, spring is on its way and spring always comes". And it did. Her next chance to flee came several weeks later.

Gloria's Father had been on an unusually long drinking binge – She suspected that he had problems at work, or maybe a co-worker? He came home more ornery and disagreeable than usual. Gloria remembered keeping a low profile since her last attempt to run away (which was never mentioned again) as not to draw any unwanted attention. This time she prepared a bag with clothes, some food and money, which she hid under the porch – then she went about her day. After school, she cared for her sister and made supper. To her surprise her father came home from work early, not to her surprise he was drunk. Supper wasn't quite finished cooking as he stumbled into the kitchen, ranting about the injustices in the world and how he was shortchanged by fate. Gloria continued cooking, when he grabbed the spoon out of her hand, tasted the soup she was cooking and with great energy spit it out, propelling it into her face. Gloria winced as she recalled "I was stunned". "Although he had acted badly many times before, this time seemed differ- ent, more vicious, more hateful, and more direct. I was really afraid" He continued the tirade by verbally degrading her, stat- ing that she was "a useless bitch like her mother and would never amount to anything more than a whore". Gloria didn't speak or look up. She bravely wiped the soup off her face and held back her tears. "I didn't want him to see me crying. I didn't want to seem weak". As usual he stumbled to his lounge chair, still chastising her cooking, threatening to "fix your scrawny ass".

Gloria had heard enough. She knew it was time to leave. So after HE passed out and the snoring started Gloria once again escaped thru the bathroom window. Down the roof and onto the ground, she grabbed her bag that was hidden under the porch and away she went. "This time I had a plan. This time I was not coming back." So she stayed off the main roads, trav- eled thru the woods and stayed out of sight. She made her way to the bus station where she looked for someone who would purchase her ticket without asking questions. Gloria recalled seeing a very busy, well dressed businessman who seemed unaware of anything but his own business. She chuckled as she remembered how she casually approached him and made a lame request for him to purchase her ticket. "I gave him the money for my fare and fortunately he seemed very preoccupied and uninterested". She recalled how he robotically purchased the ticket, and handed it to her. Thankful for the absence of conversation she clutched the ticket and within the hour was out of town.

Gazing into space Gloria collected her thoughts and focused on her story. "I rode the bus as far as it would take me, I was careful not to make eye contact with fellow travelers, so I kept a low profile. Fortunately, everyone seemed focused on themselves. It was a quiet ride with only the hum of the bus' motor lulling the travelers into a quasi hypnotic state". "When the bus finally stopped I was in a huge parking authority. There were busses and people everywhere. Everyone seemed to be moving with purpose, as if they had somewhere to go and someone to see, everyone except me". Gloria began to fidget uncomfortably as she continued her story. She recalled getting off the bus, moving thru the terminal and exiting the building. She mentioned the statue of Ralph Cramden, the fictitious character from the Honeymooners TV show stood outside the bus terminal. The figurine reminded her of the late night reruns that would play on TV as her Dad sat passed out, propped in his chair, drunk. A chill came over her as she thought about the life she left and silently she vowed never to return to that life. New York City, Manhattan, the Big Apple, and Gloria. A bag of clothes, a couple tasty cakes and less than $45 to her name, she'd never been to any city, no less New York, and had no idea where to go or what to do next. So she walked, and walked and walked.

The lights and sounds of New York City were mesmerizing. As Gloria recalled this time of her life, her time in New York was always frenzied, frantic and fretful. "I never knew what was around each corner" "the first three nights I slept on some rocks amidst some shrubs in Central Park - I hid so no one would see me -during the day I watched people throw their leftover food into the garbage and I would wait for them to leave so I could retrieve it" . Gloria recalled always moving, unsure where she was going but determined not to stay where she was. Within a week of arriving in NYC Gloria encountered a girl seemingly younger and somewhat frail and timid named Angie, who tagged along with Gloria. Gloria appeared softer and less angry when talking about Angie. "Angie had no agenda and was unsure of where she was going but she trusted me and decided to follow" Gloria continued "I remember Angie coyly asking if I knew where we were going and I was irritated that she would even ask, even though I had no idea!"

Gloria recalled being irritated to have the complication of a companion.

"I could barely feed myself and I didn't need to have another mouth to feed or another person to worry about exposing me!" Gloria could be curt and to the point and her recollection was of Angie looking hurt and disappointed. Remembering the hurt look in Angie's eyes, Gloria softened her tone. "I told her it was ok, just don't make any trouble for me and off we went to sleep under a bridge for the night"

"We were two waifs huddled together, unaware of the potential dangers surrounding us. When morning came we headed out from under the bridge which was near Central Park- and focused on food". Curious about Angie, I encouraged Gloria to tell me more about her, she complied. "Angie was a runaway from the mid-west; she basically hopped on a bus, like me to get away from her family. Angie didn't like to talk about her family anymore than I did - she would bristled when asked about her family and would simply state she never knew her dad but her mom always had a boyfriend. Angie said some were nicer than others... and had a hard time talking beyond that point. I'd see her eyes become blank and empty when talking about the last boyfriend who wouldn't leave her alone, after her mom would go to sleep he'd come into her room and force Angie to have sex with him....she told me how she tried to fight him off but he'd over power her..."

Gloria had a lot in common with Angie – especially when it came to abuse. Continuing Gloria snickered as she remembered asking Angie "why didn't you tell your mother?? Surely she would've protected you!"

Angie looked forlorn and betrayed as she revealed "No, she didn't believe me, she said I was lying and threw me out. That's why I'm here". There was nothing else to say - both girls seemed to have an unspoken understanding that words didn't need to express. Gloria remembered leaving the park and venturing downtown, toward the theater district, hoping to find some reasonable remains of a meal.

She told how the two girls walked quickly and quietly through the maze of bodies, all moving with seeming purpose and intent. Keeping stride with the commuters, who were being drawn to the midtown bus station, each commuter prepared to leave the fast pace of the city and return to the slower, safer suburbs, Angie and Gloria had no safe place to go. Both girls became dependent on the company of the other. Midtown was exciting any hour of the day or night, the neon lights, street corner barkers, all encouraging passerbyers to stop by their shop or restaurant. Gloria shook her head as if to erase the memory of always feeling hungry; readily scoping discarded food out of dumpsters, and rummaging behind restaurants for remnants of food. It was still better than being home.

Gently, I raise the question, "what went wrong? With a suspicious eye Gloria softly and slowly told me how her life on the street changed. "Summer nights in the city are different; there is a different energy, exciting yet unpredictable, thrilling yet potential volatile" Gloria took a deep breath,

"Angie and I had trouble keeping food because it spoils quicker in the summer so we had to venture into a different neighborhood in the city where we heard the food might be fresher". Hesitantly Gloria admitted they really did not know the area. "We were so excited to find food that had not become rancid we really were not aware of who was around us. All of a sudden, a group of guys approached us and wanted our food."

"They started to push us and taunt us; Angie started to cry and I threw a half eaten sandwich at one of them, hitting him directly in the face." "I'll never forget how he spun around and ran at me, grabbing me by my wrist." "I broke free, dropping the rest of the food, panic stricken to get away". "I started to run and I yelled at Angie to start running too but I was too late as one of the bigger boys grabbed her and ordered her to stop crying, but she only cried and screamed louder." "

Suddenly, Gloria stopped talking. She sat up straight, stiffened her body and placed both feet on the ground. I thought she might leave. I did not think she would continue talking even though this was the most time she ever spent in a session. To my surprise she swung her body around and threw a leg over the opposite arm of the chair, settled into the cushion as she closed her eyes, as if in a trance, and continued.

"Angie kept screaming and screaming as the biggest boy kept yelling at her to shut up. I had run almost a block away but another large boy chased me down and grabbed me. He held both my arms behind my back as I kicked and screamed, watching as three other boys started kicking and hitting Angie. I watched Angie's petite frame go limp and collapse onto the pavement. One more moan and she was quiet. Angie was dead."

Gloria wiped away a tear and paused. Collecting her emotions and thoughts Gloria continued talking in a soft monotone voice.

"When I realized Angie was dead I went crazy, I momentarily broke free and I was hitting, punching and biting anyone who touched me – the whole group of boys had turned their attack on me" Through clenched teeth Gloria began to cry – "Those boys dragged me into an ally and held me down so I couldn't move, they stuffed a piece of rotten fruit into my mouth so I couldn't yell and then, after beating me, one after the other they raped me." Gloria hesitated then added "As they were leaving each boy spit on me. Gloria hesitated, glanced across the room then looked directly at me and stated "I must have passed out because I don't remember anything else. I do remember thinking how much I hate them all". We both sat quietly. There was nothing I could say that would not sound like it came out of a textbook. Sometimes the most sensitive response is to say nothing.

As I reviewed Gloria's chart it simply stated she was hospitalized and released against medical advice. There was no indication she had been raped. Mercifully someone venturing down the ally had heard Angie's screams and called the police. They arrived too late to save Angie but just in time to help Gloria. Once at the hospital Gloria said she gave the hospital a phony name and age because she still feared being returned to her father. After three days in the hospital she signed herself out. Concerned that she had never been treated physically or mentally for the rape I asked her if she told anyone about what happened the night Angie died. She just shook her head no. "I never talked about it to anyone, ever, before now". "I returned to the streets, alone." Tears were welled up in Gloria's eyes as she fought to hold them back.

"I didn't want to admit it but I missed Angie". "I really missed her, she was like the little sister I never had, I got use to her tagging along, asking dumb questions but always following my lead; I really missed her a lot".

Gloria whimpered but held back obvious emotion. This was the most she ever revealed, to anyone and I didn't want to screw this up. Working through this kind of deep seeded trauma is like walking through a mine field. One wrong step and it can all blow up. I liked Gloria and I wanted to help her.

"Gloria?" I hesitated, knowing the question I was about to ask could be devastating "Did you become pregnant as a result of the rape? Gloria looked at me and her eyes locked onto mine, as a scornful smirk slowly crossed her face. "Is that what you think? Really? After a year of coming here week after week you think my beautiful girl is the product of a rape? Really?" Her amazed expression was almost demonic. Confused, I asked who the baby's father is and Gloria replied sardonically "not the rapist!!" Gloria then reversed her position in the chair and swung her legs back over the side. Taking a deep breath, then exhaling, Gloria stared into space as she prepared herself to speak.

"After the rape and Angie's murder I stayed away from everyone. I wandered thru the city like a stray ally cat looking for food and a dry place to sleep, what I owned I carried on my back, and I choose to stay far away from people."

Still staring into space Gloria's voice became very hushed, as if she were telling me a secret. I listened intently, saying nothing.

"Winter was coming and I needed warmer clothes, I had seen a flyer advertising free coats at the Salvation Army so I made it a point to go there and get one." "When I entered the Salvation Army a heavy set elderly woman with a friendly smile eagerly approached me

"You poor dear, you must be frozen, it's below freezing outside and that sweater you are wearing is paper thin... I have a beautiful coat that looks like it will fit you perfectly...come back here and try it on". Gloria recalled following the friendly woman to the back of the store where assorted jackets and coats were hung.

"I made some soup and I was about to have a bowl, would you like to join me? I'd really like some company" not waiting for a reply the kind woman placed a bowl of soup and a slice of fresh hot bread in front of Gloria. "I couldn't resist. I hadn't had food in a bowl, at a table, in months. I couldn't eat it fast enough" Gloria remembered how the kind lady refilled Gloria's bowl with more soup and gave her more bread. "I felt human". "After I finished eating I felt the need to move on, I took the coat that fit me perfectly, thanked the kind lady and headed toward the door. As I was leaving I heard her yell, "What's your name? " "I replied Gloria". "The last thing I heard was her yelling that her name was Grace, and I should stop back again". As was her custom, Gloria vanished into the night.

"It wasn't too long after that visit that I went back to the Salvation Army, I would always look for Grace. Grace was always kind and friendly. She was my friend. When I would come into the store she would always find something new for me to wear and something warm to eat. I started to look forward to our visits" "Grace never asked any questions about my life and that made me feel safe." Glaring at me, realizing she had already told me more than she had intended she decided to continue her story. "Grace became my only friend and as time went on she started to give me work at the Salvation Army. Soon Grace even let me sleep in a backroom, I was officially off the street! I worked hard, but I didn't mind because she was so kind and generous."

Gloria's tone changed as she spoke of Grace and the Salvation Army store. She looked more relaxed, less stressed and carefree. Her words seemed more candid and less contrived. "Several times a month Grace and I would take some of the surplus clothing to a shelter on the other side of the city. It wasn't uncommon for shelters and thrift stores like the Salvation Army to swap clothing, food or other necessities. Most of the trips were uneventful" … Gloria's voice trailed off as she seemed to day dream about a happier time. "I knew everyone who worked at the shelter until one day there was someone new. Everyone called him Ryno, but his real name was Ryan." For the first time I could ever remember Gloria looked youthful, not jaded or hard; her expression was that of a smitten school girl. Ryno, apparently was someone special. "We spent a lot of time together through the spring and summer, He made me laugh and I felt safe and special when I was with him" Gloria became guarded and reluctant to say any thing more or less about Ryno. It was clear he was special to her. "When August came Ryno left for college. At first we wrote to each other but as the weeks went by we drifted apart." "I found out I was pregnant sometime in October, but I never told Ryno, I didn't want to be a burden." Gloria's expression turned to pain. It was very apparent Ryno was very important to her as she held back the tears and finished her story.

"So here I am, 3 years later and the mother of a toddler. Ryno never went back to work at the shelter and we haven't had any contact since that summer 3 years ago. Grace is helping me raise my daughter." Gloria paused as if to signal the end of that topic. "Now you know everything. Are we done? I really don't have anything else to say. My daughter Angie Grace will be waking up from her nap and I need to be there." As if to punctuate this statement Gloria stood up, walked toward the door, turned the knob then turned around and politely asked

"Same time next week?" and I replied

"Yes, same time next week"

The law enforcement code of ethics reads as follows:

As a law enforcement officer, my fundamental duty is to serve mankind; to safeguard lives and property; to protect the innocent against deception, the weak against oppression or intimidation, and the peaceful against violence or disorder; and to respect the Constitutional rights of all persons to liberty, equality and justice.

I will keep my private life unsullied as an example to all; maintain courageous calm in the face of danger, scorn or ridicule; develop self-restraint; and be constantly mindful of the welfare of others. Honest in thought and deed in both my personal and official life, I will be exemplary in obeying the laws of the land and the regulations of my department. Whatever I see or hear of a confidential nature or that is confided to me in my official capacity will be kept ever secret unless revelation is necessary in the performance of my duty.

I will never act officiously or permit personal feelings, prejudices, animosities or friendships to influence my decisions. With no compromise for crime and with relentless prosecution of criminal, I will enforce the law courteously and appropriately without fear or favor, malice or ill will, never employing unnecessary force or violence and never accepting gratuities.

I recognize the badge of my office as a symbol of public faith, and I accept it as a public trust to be held so long as I am true to the ethics of the police service. I will constantly strive to achieve these objectives and ideals, dedicating myself before God to my chosen profession — law enforcement.

To Serve and Protect...

*T*he day I was sworn in as a police offer was the proudest day of my life. My dad, Thomas, and my grandfather, Frank Jr., had been police officers. My Dad sat in the front row of my swearing in. I was young, physically fit and mentally sound. I was ready to uphold the law and defend my community. I was ready to serve and protect.

There was never any doubt or question that I was going to be in law enforcement. My great grandfather, Frank Sr., traveled, as a young boy, to NYC as an Irish immigrant. It was during the mid 1800's, when immigrants from Ireland, most were refugees from the great potato famine, came to America. Leaving behind his family and a country filled with despair he snuck onto a cargo ship, bound for New York. The Irish packed into the holds of the ships where filth and disease were rampant. They slept on narrow, closely stacked shelves and headed toward this land of great opportunity. The Irish began settling on the west side of Manhattan in a section known as Hell's Kitchen. My father would tell me and my siblings' stories about the early housing which were called shanty towns or slum settlements. Impoverished people, mostly immigrants, like my family, would learn to call this home. Fistfights over clothesline rights or all out drunken brawls with ax handles and clubs were common. You grew up fast in Hell's Kitchen – and your future was decided early, good or bad, you made the choice. Men, like my great grandfather Frank Sr. worked hard labor for pennies a day. He was gone from dawn to dusk and life was dismal. Hell's Kitchen was a few blocks from the Hudson River and it was here that my great grandfather, Frank Sr, found work on the docks. My dad would tell stories about how proud the men in our family were to work everyday and earn an honest day's wages. My great grandfather was considered lucky as many immigrants could not find work. I grew up proud of our family work ethic and our ability to provide for the family. Other, less honorable men looked for fast cash by gambling, running numbers, burglary and muggings.

New York has always had gangs. During my Great Grandfather Frank's time the Gophers and Westies (The name—used by the press and the police, not by the mobsters themselves) were the Irish Mob. These were gangs made up of Irish Immigrants or new Irish Americans. The Irish Mob's activities were less than wholesome and not law abiding. My great grandfather Frank was never one to fear anyone, but he did not look for trouble either. He had his daily routine and minded his own business. Part of his routine was to stop at the Irish American Social Club, a quiet local bar where everyone knew each other and neighbors gathered to exchange daily news and share gossip. He would

stop every day on his way home from the docks for "a shot of
Irish and a beer" and then walk home. It was a common belief
that a man who worked hard, drank hard. Whiskey was a working man's reward and a poor man's solace. As was his routine
he would leave the bar precisely at 6:00pm, be home by 6:20
and dinner was on the table by 6:30. Neighbors would comment "it must be 6:20 cause Frank just got home". One particular evening 6:20 came and went and no sign of great grand
father Frank. 7:00, 7:30 came and went as the family became
anxious knowing this was completely out of the norm. Fearful
that an accident may have happened on the dock, my great
grand mother sent her oldest son, my grandfather, Frank Jr., to
the dock for information about his father. Frank Jr. the oldest of
6 children and the only boy enthusiastically ran out the door
eager to see his father and walk home with him. All the children adored their father but because of his long hours at work
and need for rest when he was home they did not spend much
time with him. Frank Jr. saw this as an opportunity to have his
father all to himself- if only for the short walk home. Frank Jr.
walked the route that his father walked to the dock only to find
his father, with blood splattering from his head laying face
down in an ally. His body had been brutally beaten, a blood
soaked bat laid near his body. Frank Jr. ran to get help but it was
too late - his father was dead. Rumors spread and most specu-
lated that the murder was initiated by the Westies who had mistaken Great Grand father Frank for a snitch. A simple case of
mistaken identity ended Frank's life. The newly formed New
York City Police Department (NYPD), established in 1845, did
not have the experience or manpower to investigate this murder.
No one was ever arrested. Such started our family legacy of law
enforcement as Frank Jr. decided that day to become a police
officer.

Frank Jr. and his son, my father, Thomas, both were decorated police officers. Their careers were exemplary. They had
worked the same precinct, walked the same beat, proud of the
NYPD. There was never any question what I would do when I
grew up -I wanted to carry out the family tradition so I too,

entered the police academy and law enforcement. My grandfather, now deceased, and my father, now retired, set the family standard for ethical and moral action. Police work was in my blood and I wanted to make my family proud.

I completed the academy and graduated at the top of my class. I was sworn in as a NYC Police Officer and was given an investigative assignment for the first 18 months. It wasn't long that I was promoted from Police Officer to Detective-Investigator. Detective-investigators are assigned to specialized units at either the major command or citywide level and I was assigned to investigate narcotics dealing. It was even more exciting as I was going to be working undercover. The prospect of investigating illegal drug deals and being an undercover detective was the challenge I was looking for. My life was complete; I belonged to a respected family, I had a career I loved, and a wonderful girl I adored who I recently married. I never thought life could change so quickly.

Trudy, my wife and best friend understood me better than anyone. We had known each other since high School. She knew how career driven I was and how important police work was to me. She knew I wanted to impress my father by doing well and she was proud of me. We had a comfortable apartment not far from the precinct. Trudy was a RN and was fortunate to work steady day shift. We were making good money and saving to buy a house and start a family. She understood the dangers of undercover work but also knew my need to excel and be challenged.

Working undercover presented many challenges and changes to my life - As an uniformed officer I had always had strict scheduling and a regimented lifestyle. I no longer had to meet many of the uniformed officers regulations - I explained to my wife the importance of separating from the department, the theory behind not wearing a uniform, that it was easier to acquire information if I looked less formidable, less like a cop. I didn't have to cut my hair or shave as part of my new persona. I could wear street clothes and didn't have to attend mandatory department meetings -I was no longer working as a team -even my partner Dave, wasn't always aware of where I was or what I was doing. I was able to take on an assumed identity/persona for an unspecified but significant amount of time. I understood the importance and necessity of the police officer to be able to circulate in areas where the uniformed police are not ordinarily welcome.

My work sounded simple. As an undercover officer I was to "make cases", in other words, to gather enough information to enable a successful prosecution. I had to obtain physical evidence (by purchasing drugs or other contraband) and become the complainant seeking an arrest warrant. Within a short time I was arresting many street level dealers. The old buy-and-bust operations aimed at dealers on the street stopped being a challenge. My superior officers were very pleased with my work and encouraged me to seek out higher volume manufacturing distribution operations. I agreed.

I was relishing my new found freedom even though undercover work presented different problems at home. One of the problems was that undercover work required secrecy. I couldn't share any of my activities with Trudy, which made life very tense. We couldn't plan ahead, even simple dinners out had to be out of town or not at all. To keep her safe we weren't seen anywhere in public together. Another problem was my work wasn't regular shift work - I worked mostly nights and those hours were unpredictable. Trudy worked straight days. I would sleep late in the morning because I was working late at night and most of my work focused in bars and clubs. It made being with my wife difficult and many nights it was easier and safer for her if I didn't come home at all. Trudy would ask for details and I couldn't provide them. Our relationship became distanced. I couldn't share any of my work with her and she lost patience in waiting for me. We were going in different directions. After a short time I moved out and onto the street.

This was a perfect undercover cover. I was living on the street focused on bring down the local crack manufacturer/distribution hub. I was tired and hungry when I ran into several local junkies looking for a fix.

"Humm, typical junkies" I thought to myself, observing worn, layered clothes too big for their skin and bones bodies.

"You got any junk?" one eagerly asked, obviously jonesing for a fix

"Nope, I'm looking for some crack, know where I can score?"

"Yeah", said a little nervous voice in the shadows, "down in Washington Square there's a chick looking to get rid of some"
"She's got long black hair and white skin, really white skin; she goes by the name Snowbird."

"Really? Snowbird?? Whatever..." I chuckled at the irony,

"Who should I say sent me?"

"Iggy"

Thanks, Iggy, I'll look for her" and off I went.

Thinking back, I don't know when I began to lose perspective.   I became emotionally attached to undercover work. I don't mean that I became emotionally attached to the suspects, I was attached to the singleness of my work - it was just me against the world. I began to feel insecure and anxious about regular police work and questioned whether I would continue employment with the department. I even questioned whether I really wanted to be a cop. Criminality can be intoxicating.

Nine plus acres makes up Washington Square Park, yet Snowbird was easy to find. She stood under the large marble Washington Arch at the entrance to the park. As foretold by Iggy, Snowbird had long black hair and white skin, really white skin, which made her stand out from the crowd. I approached her cautiously as not to make her fearful or guarded, but she was neither. I asked if she knew a place where I could crash. Snowbird never questioned who or where I came from - she wrote down an address and handed it to me - then vanished into the crowd. I had stopped wearing any police issued gear when I first went undercover. No gun, no vest, no badge. I had a knife in my sock but that was it. I went to the address that Snowbird gave me and it was a run down abandoned building. No one was around as I went in, stepping over broken glass and assorted fast food wrappers. I could hear eerie laughter coming from somewhere in the building but could not see any faces. I found an area where several bodies were laying around, and the room felt like death. I could see shallow breathing on a couple of the bodies but no one was moving. It was creepy. I saw a corner which was not occupied so I huddled there, and attempted to sleep. What seemed like only a matter of moments I heard voices yelling- screaming

"GET UP!! GET UP!! WHO THE FUCK ARE YOU?????????" confused and disoriented I respond "SNAKE (my street name) from uptown, Iggy sent me and Snowbird gave me this address".

"WHAT THE FUCK DO YOU WANT??" "SNAKE? WHO THE HELL ARE YOU?? "

"I told you, Iggy sent me - I just needed a place to crash ..."

"Leave him alone, Herme, He's with me" said Snowbird now moving closer to Herme.

Herme was not relived that Snowbird was vouching for me. His deep set dark bloodshot eyes peered out from under a knit skull cap that was pulled down over his ears and covered part of his face.

"WHAT DO YOU WANT?" he asked suspiciously, as he wiped his runny nose on his sleeve.

"I just want to crash - get the fuck away from me" I stated, looking at Herme, waiting for a response.

Turning to Snowbird, Herme yelled at her "I told you not to bring anyone new here unless I SAY it's ok, cops are everywhere and I'M NOT doing more time because of a stupid bitch." Snowbird did not seem fazed as she looked at Herme and calmly asked for a cigarette. I was impressed with her lack of reaction to Herme's ranting. Still ranting about the dangers of bringing strangers into their house Herme became distracted by a loud disturbance in another room and he left abruptly. Snowbird sat next to me, lit her cigarette and inhaled deeply. Neither of us spoke as we watched smoke rings disappear into the darkness.

Days and nights blended together at Herme's house. At first I just slept and stayed out of the way, but Herme would not tolerate anyone not pulling their weight. Herme seemed to have an eye on me even though we didn't really cross paths. After several days of successful avoidance Herme cornered me. "Hey Snake - Come here, I got something to show you - What do you think??" Herme revealed two large crystal cocaine rocks "one for you and one for me... What do you say Snake? You game? Herme watched my expression looking for the slightest indication that I would refuse. "Light 'um up" I said with absolute confidence, aware that my cover would be blown if I did not participate. The Crack was consumed incredibly fast. My first smoke was an amazing high. My desire to use more crack defied self control and will power. My desire to recapture that same level of high overcame me; So much so I wanted to smoke more and more of the drug in a very short period of time. Intellectually I knew this could get out of hand very very quickly - it did not matter. I wanted more. I knew it was not uncommon for someone to spend several hundred dollars on the drug, and then end up smoking all of it within a few hours. "I'm a police officer, I can control it" I thought to myself. Other people might go out again and again the same day and spend hundreds more on crack. They will keep spending and spending until it is all gone. "But not me, I'm a trained professional".

Soon I was taking cash advances on my credit card and buying rocks. Trudy had not seen me or heard from me in months so she canceled my credit cards and reported my bank cards stolen. The police department no longer had control of me and I knew the department's integrity was compromised by my behavior. Occasionally I would listen to my department voicemail where I was repeatedly requested to report for duty. The department made futile attempts to salvage my usefulness as a regular police officer. It was to no avail. It was too late. I had already become a rogue cop - paranoid and untrusting of everyone. Herme's crack house had now become my home.

Without realizing, I had morphed into the very being I despised. No longer did I represent law and order but instead I was the epitome of lawlessness. I had lost my athletic build and now appeared gaunt and grey. My hair was long and shaggy. My normally clean shaven face now sported a patchy, unkempt beard. Hygiene wasn't a concern. Like Herme, I was suspicious of anyone new visiting or staying in our house. I was often irritable, restless and unhappy with everyone. Most of my day was spent trying to score cocaine to make more crack. I was making crack, then smoking crack, before selling crack to buy more cocaine - It was an endless cycle that was now my life. The high was short but glorious. The low was long and miserable.

Herme maintained a suspicious eye on anyone new in the house or in the neighborhood, including me. We weren't friends just using buddies. As time went by I became careless - all I wanted was to get high and I was forever chasing the perfect high. I started smoking crack and marijuana together - oolies, and dealing marijuana for additional cash. I heard on the street that there was a guy in the neighborhood who was interested in making a large purchase of crack. I was eager to turn over some product and a large hit would spare me multiple trips out of the house. I decided to meet with the guy. As I approached our pre-determined meeting place I thought nothing of the attention drawn to this deal. Everyone on the street seemed to know about it. The guy I was making the deal with looked vaguely familiar, but I did not give it much thought. I was too eager to make the deal and get back to the house and get high. Unsure of where I knew him from I sold a substantial amount of crack to him. Pleased with the score, I returned to our house, unaware that he was watching where I was going. Within a very short amount of time there was a banging on the door

"Police, we have a warrant!" before I knew what was happening several uniformed officers entered the crack house, grabbed me as I was thrown down on the ground- Other addicts scattered but the police did not seem interested in them.

"Are you Brett Kelly??" "I am" I muttered under my breath.

"That's him" I heard another officer yell. "That's the one I bought the crack from"

Now I remembered, the neighborhood guy who looked familiar and bought the crack was another undercover cop -

My past life memories flooded my thoughts, I remembered my police training, my family history of police work, my wife Trudy, somehow they seemed very real as I saw my police partner Dave in the group of uniformed cops.

It is indescribable the shame and guilt I felt as the cuffs were placed on my wrists. My partner, Dave, turned and looked away as not to make eye contact with me. As we exited the crack house, even the crack whores loathed me. Snowbird, with long black hair and white skin, really white skin, spit on the ground before me. I had betrayed everyone, my job, my family, my fellow officers, the crack addicts I hung with. I repulsed everyone. The sunlight hurt my eyes and I shielded myself from the onslaught of journalists, and camera men asking a million questions. Into the backseat of the patrol car I sat and away we went to be processed. My father met us at the police station. We hadn't seen each other in many months and I knew this reunion was not going to be easy for either one of us.

"How you doing?" I asked him, but he just shook his head and looked away.

I tried again "Thanks for coming here" still no acknowledgement, just a long painful silence.

One more try "How's Mom?" that was it.

He exploded, shouting at the top of his voice "How do YOU think SHE is?" "YOU think SHE needed any of this????" "First she feared you were dead and then this....?."

"YOU think she needed to hear that her only son is a double-crossing good for nothing drug addict?" "You betrayed me, your mother, the department, and your fellow officers"

a long silent pause and then he looked me straight in the eye and said with absolute clarity "you are a disgrace and a humiliation to this family and your badge" "This bail money is the last money you will ever get from me and your mother and this conversation is the last time we will ever speak" Is that clear??? I mouthed the words "Yes, sir" but not a sound came out. No one at the station said a word - everyone in Manhattan had to have heard my father and no one dared say a word. My Father turned his back to me, signed some paperwork, and walked out of the precinct. It would be the last time I would ever see him. Dave methodically unlocked my handcuffs, gave me some paperwork to sign, mumbled something about appearing in court and court appointed lawyer but I wasn't listening. All I kept hearing was my father's last words, "you are a disgrace; a humiliation to this family and your badge"" you are a disgrace; a humiliation to this family and your badge"" you are a disgrace; a humiliation to this family and your badge". I left the precinct knowing I could never return.

I walked 10 blocks to Trudy's apartment. I rang the buzzer but no one answered. I was glad that Trudy wasn't home and grateful to see after all this time she still left the key hidden under the matt. I went in. Nothing had changed; the apartment was just as I remembered. It was if I had never left -" maybe she was waiting for me? Nawh, she would never take me back - I was glad she wasn't home -I couldn't stand to see the disappointment in her eyes, seeing my father had been enough.." I started to cry but held back the tears - Again his words ripped thru me like a bullet "you are a disgrace; a humiliation to this family and your badge". Frantic to end the miserable mantra, I went into the bedroom and bellied under the bed - groping anxiously I found the wooden box that held my Smith & Wesson 9mm service pistol - "Always one bullet in the chamber, I released the safety, put the barrel in my mouth and pulled the trigger..."

Mark's last Bogie

"Perhaps I should have told you sooner..... I wasn't sure how you'd handle this but I've to tell someone... everything I say is confidential, right? I can trust you....right?

"Yes, Mark, we've been thru this before, Do I need to explain Doctor/ patient confidentiality again? "

Mark shook his head indicating it wasn't necessary.

Every weekly session started the same, Mark needing reassurance, Dr.Showden providing it.

"Ok, let's begin," hummmmm "I see your drug screen was positive for Methamphetamines" Dr.Showden's voice trailed off as he became more absorbed in reading the drug screen results than talking to Mark.

"Mark, your drug screen has been positive 6 out of the last 10 tests, can you explain why that is?" Dr. Showden's tone was calm yet direct.

"That's what I have to tell you, it's killing me doc, I gotta tell someone or I'll go crazy... I should've told you sooner.... "

"Mark, you do realize that continued drug use warrants a higher level of care, in your case inpatient treatment, are you prepared to do inpatient treatment?"

Mark appeared agitated; scratching and twitching randomly, his eyes darting around the room.

"no, no I can't do inpatient, I have to tell you something important and then you'll understand.."

Sitting back in his chair, Dr. Showden put Mark's chart on the side table, adjusted his glasses and settled in for Mark's disclosure.

"I'm an informant - I'm working for Cambria County vice squad as a paid informant, I have been for 3 months and I'm not supposed to tell anyone... no one knows. Gazing over his glasses, his expression never changing Dr. Showden matter-of-factly continued the conversation.

"What about your parole officer? He must know ...Dr. Showden paused and waited for a response. Mark, looking anxious said nothing as Dr. Showden casually commented "Mark - Who do you report to? And what kind of work are you doing?" Suspicious of this new explanation for Mark's apparent drug use, Dr. Showden selectively questioned Mark who appeared eager to abide.

Mark was more than just a meth addict. Mark had been a semi-professional golf pro but had taken too much of a liking to the false sense of energy that Meth provided. His boyish charm and competitive edge made him a favorite amongst the country club set. Small in stature his gregarious personality filled a room. As meth became more and more a part of Mark's life he drifted away from that social circle. The side effects from his use of meth included tremors, irritability and confusion which ultimately destroyed his golf game and career. The additional side effect of being arrested and incarcerated ultimately destroyed his family and reputation. As part of his parole, Mark was court ordered into intensive outpatient drug and alcohol treatment and Mark's initial response to mandated treatment was hesitant and resistant. After several sessions Mark became comfortable with Dr. Showden and appeared to enjoy the attention that individual therapy provided. Mark liked to keep therapy light and superficial so this sudden sense of urgency was unprecedented. Dr. Showden permitted Mark to set the pace for this session as Mark continued.

"Cambria County approached me when I was being released from prison - They suggested I help them, considering my vast contacts in the drug manufacturing business"

Dr. Showden held back the urge to smirk and thought to himself, "drug manufacturing business? Humph, It sounds almost legitimate..." Mark was rattling on, obviously impressed with his own inflated sense of importance as Dr.Showden interrupted,

"So, you are saying that Cambria County hired you to report on people you previously purchased drugs from in an effort to arrest them??"Yea, yea that's it" Mark seemed relived that his secret was out. "You're the only person I've told Doc, now you know why I can't pass a drug test..." Dr. Showden hesitated, giving a great deal of thought to how he would respond to that statement.

"Mark, you do realize this poise a problem regarding your recovery - If everything you have told me is true, and that is IF I can collaborate your story; let's say you are an informant and you have been using drugs as a way to gain the trust of the dealer. In your attempt to purchase drugs so the vice squad can shut them down, you used drugs; so technically, you are not clean or sober." Mark's expression changed from relief to frustration.

"But I'm doing the right thing, I'm helping shut down meth labs, I'm working with the police..." Mark's pleading was reminiscent of when he first entered treatment, trying to convince Dr. Showden that he only used meth once and got caught..." Mark did not have a history of being honest or consistent and his stories changed weekly. The current drug test also raised questions of doubt. Dr. Showden collected his thoughts then carefully phrased them in such a way as not to alienate Mark but hopefully extract a level of earnestness.

"It appears to me that you are in a quandary" "on one hand you say you want to be clean and sober yet on the other hand you want to work for the drug vice squad and shut down the meth labs. "Mark nodded enthusiastically believing his drug use was being validated by Dr. Showden whom he respected and whose approval he sought.

"Mark, we've got a problem, you are a drug addict - and anything you put before your recovery you are going to loose -" Mark listened intently, hoping to hear praise for his work with the drug vice squad. The praise did not come "You're playing Russian roulette with your life; on so many levels this is dangerous" "Can you see where you might have a moral conflict?" Mark looked genuinely stymied and did not respond. Being an informant solved many of his problems, first and foremost it made him financially solvent, secondly he felt respectable, after all it's ok to snitch on the bad guys....thirdly, as much as he didn't want to admit it he could continue using and get high on the county's dime. .. Recovery and abstinence was somewhere off in the future.

Dr. Showden still was not convinced Mark really was an informant. Mark couldn't produce a contact person or any documentation confirming his role as informant. "Could Mark really be that cunning and crafty to create this chronicle of espionage and intrigue? " Dr. Showden wasn't sure.

A week went by since Mark's last appointment with Dr.Showden. As usual Mark arrived on time for his session.

"Doc? About last week's session, everything is confidential right?

"Yes Mark, Do I need to explain Doctor/ patient confidentiality again? "

Mark shook his head indicating it wasn't necessary. Dr. Showden Cleared his throat and began

"Mark, your drug test came back positive for methamphetrhines, I'm going to refer you for inpatient treatment". A long Silence and then Mark shot out of his chair as if his rear were on fire " The hell I am - I told you why I'm dirty for meth, weren't you listening? If I go inpatient I can't continue working as an informant - If my PO knows I'm dirty he'll violate me and send me back to jail. Doc, I trusted you, you can't send me inpatient or tell my P.O" Mark was pleading for the impossible. Ethically, Dr. Showden could not continue treating Mark at this level of care while he continued using and he still was convinced that Mark's use was more than rouge for the vice squad. Mark suddenly became quiet, as if to collect his thoughts before launching into his next defense. His eyes kept darting back and forth, between Dr. Showden, and the exit. Mark was obviously agitated. "ok Doc, do what you have to do, but if something bad happens to me its all on you" Dr. Showden looked directly at Mark with an expression of half humor and half disgust, "Now Mark, lets look at that last statement, do you really believe that I am responsible for your fate? Mark lets look at the choices YOU made that got YOU where YOU are today"

Mark's attempt to guilt the doctor into changing his mind had failed. "Ok, Ok, I know it's my fault, but I don't need inpatient care - I got this under control - I just need to finish working undercover this one last time and I'll stop using forever." Mark's request seemed feeble and far-fetched. Dr. Showden was not in the mood to negotiate. "Mark, Your drug use is out of control, regardless of your work with the vice squad, you are a drug addict using drugs - it's that simple " "I'm referring you to inpatient and I'm going to have to inform your PO". "After you successfully complete inpatient care you are more than welcome to resume outpatient treatment with me". Mark nodded, apparently resigned to this turn of events. "Hey Doc, would it be ok if I tell my PO? You know, let him hear it from me? "Dr. Showden agreed as he dialed Mark's PO number and handed the phone to Mark. Mark, matter-of-factly told his PO about being hot for methamphetamine and working for the vice squad. Without his usual flair for drama, Mark agreed to wait at Dr. Showden's office until his PO could stop by to talk. Mark hung up the phone and looked at Dr. Showden "hope you are happy doc",

"It's not about being happy, it's about doing the right thing"

"yeah yeah whatever....." Mark slumped down in his chair and closed his eyes, apparently done with Dr. Showden. Within the hour, Mark's PO arrived. Once again, Mark tried to align someone in authority into his chaotic world. The PO listened intently, nodding and appearing to agree with Mark. Then, unexpectedly he asked Mark to turn around, Mark agreed as the PO asked him to put his hands behind his back, and he cuffed Mark.

"What the hell are you doing? We're working on the same side - "Mark appeared genuinely confused as the PO explained "Mark, there has been a warrant out for your arrest for violating your parole; Starting with possession, manufacturing, distribution of a controlled substance ...and several new charges including impersonating/ misrepresenting oneself as law enforcement." Mark's body became limp as he struggled to stand upright. "You got to be kidding? Right? This is a joke right? Come on doc - say something..."

Dr. Showden stood by stoic and solemn, saying nothing as Mark was escorted out of the building. Dr. Showden sadly and silently acknowledged that inpatient would have been a better alternative to prison but the time for that was long past. Mark was into his fantasy version of life enhanced by excessive and extensive drug use. Dr. Showden watched from his window as Mark and his PO walked down the sidewalk toward the unmarked car. Suddenly there was a burst of loud sounds, like a car's exhaust backfiring, but it was the sound of a gun rapid firing. Unsure of which direction it was coming from, Dr. Showden ducked only to rise when the air was quiet again. Looking around relived that the office and staff were safe, Dr. Showden exhaled. Suddenly remembering why he was looking outside he redirected his focus back to the sidewalk, where laid Mark; his PO by his side desperately trying to stop Mark's bleeding. Mark had been shot. People just didn't get shot in this neighborhood, never. Mark's bloody, bullet riddled body was a first. People gathered, some to help some out of curiosity. The PO, up to his elbows in Marks blood, worked tirelessly to keep Mark alive while he impatiently awaited the EMT's. It was too late, Mark was dead. Dr. Showden looked away as the PO shook his head confirming Mark's demise. The EMT's arrived, methodically covering Mark's lifeless body and placing him in a black body bag. Mark's struggle was over.

"Good Better Best"
"Never let it Rest"
"Let the Good get Better"
"Let the Better get Best"

—Unknown

Picture Perfect Family

"Ok, so let's see what you're made of"

Report card day was my most dreaded day as a child. Grade school, Middle school, high School, it was all the same. And this report card would be no different. I knew that my fate was sealed in that 5x7 brown envelope. This was my last summer before my senior year of High School and the final report card for the school year. More pressure than ever with college visits, applications and interviews. ..

As he tore open the top of the envelope I believe I stopped breathing, watching as he methodically and calculatingly prepared for the task at hand. With the precession of a seasoned surgeon he removed the report card from the envelope "hummm, A, A, A minus?, you'll have to work on that, A, A, Beeee plusssss??????? What's that about? Slacking off? You know I don't tolerate slackers! Is that your best work? a B+ ?? I am really disappointed in this report card! How do you expect to amount to anything with a B+? You'll never get into a decent college..." his voice trailed off as he continued reading the teacher comments - all which were positive, supportive and upbeat. I knew the teachers liked me and they knew how hard I worked at my school work. Yet, his focus remained on the one and only B+ -

" I don't know what I'm going to do with you... perhaps you can take a summer class to raise that grade", suddenly sounding optimistic, knowing confidently this imperfection could be fixed, he restated his new plan " yes, that will do it, summer school, you'll get that B+ raised to an A and your report card will be perfect". "Yes, absolutely Perfect".

Being the oldest child in a picture perfect family was no easy task. My parent's wrote the rule book of what made a picture perfect family perfect and had it memorized. This mystical book contained misguided, antiquated information that they could embellish to suit each individual scenario or situation. They knew exactly how things should look and sound IF everything was to be perfect. And damn it everything would be perfect! If fate somehow denied my parents perfection they would manipulate the galaxy and make perfection happen. Control was ultimately theirs.

Realistically, I always knew Fate had nothing to do with my parents union. Every action was premeditated and planned, nothing impromptu or impulsive. Nothing was ever left to chance. First and foremost (after marriage) there must be children. A picture perfect family does not exist without children. And ideally the first child must be a male and must be born between 9 and 12 months post marriage. Given the 50/50 odds that the child might be female and being prepared for the worst possibility the anxious couple concocted a back up plan. If, they were unfortunate enough to have a female first child they would conceive another child as soon as possible. As fate would have it my parents first child was born on a beautiful warm summer day and to their chagrin the child was a healthy robust baby girl, ironically born on father's day. Disappointed yet undaunted the determined couple set their sites on producing yet another child - certainly the second child would be male.

Once again, another girl. My father was inconsolable, no male heir and not one but two baby girls. Sure they were healthy and happy but they weren't male. My mother, weak from two very close pregnancies and two c-sections was ready to do her part. As soon as she could be impregnated again, she was. And the anxiety mounted. The pregnancy was not an easy one and my mother took to her bed for most of the nine months- a place she would "take to" many times in the future. Unfortunately for her, this child was also a female. No amount of cooing and smiling could relieve my father's sorrow - another baby girl! "Damn it all ". Disappointed but undaunted dad resolved to try yet again for the son he desperately yearned for.

Finally, 9 months to the day my father's wish was fulfilled. He was elated with the birth of a son. A small, scrawny, sickly son, but a son all the same. Mother's health was seriously compromised as a result of this last pregnancy and she was told she could have no more children. My father was too excited with the birth of his son to hear how ill his wife had become. His prayers had been answered! A son and heir. Humorously, one would wonder heir to what? Our modest home and lifestyle certainly did not warrant more than a basic bequest.

Four children all under the age of three provided endless work for our not so healthy mother. A nanny was added to this awkward cast of characters so the girls would be given adequate attention and mother adequate rest. Mother tried her best to equalize the care of all her children but from his birth her little boy would require most of her attention. Mother's health was seriously compromised by the birth of her forth and last child but she persevered.

Unlike the robust healthy female children that preceded him, Richard Jacob Radenhausen III (aka RJ) was not a lively child. Jaundice at birth he required hours in the sun to help stimulate his liver. He had terrible colic and cried constantly. He was underweight, with legs that bowed out, and had a profile that resembled a rat. RJ's sisters found him to be a curiosity but were forbidden by their parents from touching or holding him out of their fear that the girls would hurt him. RJ, was a demanding baby and remained demanding as he grew up.

RJ grew into a gangly teenager. Not particularly attractive and very standoffish RJ had few friends. Although he mastered control of his doting parents before the age of 2, he never released them from life long servitude. As a baby he would whimper and they would instantly appear; as a teenager he would yell and they would materialize. No obstacle was too high, no meeting too important, no conversation worth having if RJ required his parents attention. The three little Radenhausen girls grew up adequately cared for but not nurtured. Yet each of the girls was quite talented. One was artistic and could draw beautiful sketches; another was very technological and wanted to be an engineer. I was a natural student, my love of learning made school effortless. Yet my father viewed my educational successes and my siblings' success with a suspicious and cynical eye. And any achievement was automatically put second to whatever RJ was doing. It was as if our success somehow diminished RJ's existence. Sadly, three little girls were pushed aside, dismissed and forgotten when RJ was present. Nothing accomplished by the girls, no matter how fantastic or fabulous, could win their father's favor compared to RJ's sheer existence. As children, none of RJ's sisters resented him; we loved him and wanted to be close to him. He couldn't help that he was sickly and a male, both traits which made him very special in his parents eyes. It was as if his specialness separated him from his sisters since they were obviously not treated equal. The value of daughters was only in how they contributed to being picture perfect. And any diversion from being picture perfect would be met with father's wrath.

It was the summer before I started High School that our mother quietly and peacefully died in her sleep. I often thought the demands of maintaining a picture perfect family sucked the weakened life from her frail body. Her death changed everything for this picture perfect family. My sisters and I had grown accustom to being the back drop to our brother's life. He was center stage and we were there to take up space. Our mother tried her hardest to make life equal for her children but she was not emotionally or physically strong enough to challenge our father. After she died it was as if my sisters and I too, had died. Our father made sure we were cared for but he had no interest in us. My father's only joy was our brother.

We knew he loved us but he did not value us.

It was during that same year, after my mother's death, that I realized not only was I a good student but I was also a very good athlete.   My Father's love of tennis became my love as I desperately wanted to connect with this seemingly complicated man. I would practice for hours hitting a ball against the garage wall, getting stronger and more agile each day. Finally feeling confident in my ability I asked my father to a match. Surprised that I was so confident to challenge the master, he laughed and said "well why not". I was thrilled, finally some common ground, a common interest with my aloft father. It was the next day we met on the tennis court. Not realizing that our objectives were different I naively served the first ball. Immediately I knew this was no ordinary game. There was no volley, no friendly exchange of shots; he slammed the ball and scored- I knew he had a powerful continental grip and forehand but I never expected to be met with such an aggressive assault. Prepared to play a friendly game of tennis I realized immediately that this was no friendly game. My father was going to show me who was the top dog in tennis and make sure I knew it was him. Sharing his competitive spirit I also engaged in the aggressive exchange of volleys. Back and forth both of us racing after the ball; to the net then back to the baseline. The first game he won and second game was mine. Always within 1 scoring point of each other we pressed on. The third and last game of the set we both were sweating but equally prepared to win. Neither of exchanged any civilities, this game was as serious as Wimbleton. I served the ball and after a fast volley I pulled off a chip and charge scoring successfully. In the lead I aggressively continued playing, confident that I could win the match and win my father's approval. The game was tied when after an aggressive volley my father changed his strategy jamming the ball directly at me. Unable to return the volley, I missed the ball and the win was his. Sorry to have lost but pleased to have given it my all I proudly approached the net to shake my father's hand. I was feeling pleased to have played a good game, even though I lost the set. I remember seeing his face, smiling, actually looking me, eye to eye, a look I had yearned for all of my life. I thought he was proud of me and I was happier than I ever thought I could be. Instead, as he shook my hand (as is customary after a match) the critique began.

"Better work on that backhand, it looked a little flimsy; and your serve could use some work too. You should be stronger than that with all the time you spend practicing; when I was your age I could beat people twice your age" my handshake became limp as my heart sank oblivious to my disappointment father continued

"Even your little brother has a better follow thru than you do; jamming never throws him off; you should watch HIS game". Adding a final reprimand he stated "I thought you said you were practicing everyday? Maybe tennis isn't your sport"

I was emotionally devastated. My amazement stemmed from the realization that no matter what the event, his precious son was first and foremost in his thoughts. His boy was not going to be bested by a girl, no less his sister. RJ didn't have to even be present, or even make an attempt to compete because father would make sure no one would or could out do his son. We were not one family unit, united against the world but rather separate camps fighting each other for survival. Tennis was never the same to me, my desire to play had vanished, and I was beginning to hate RJ simply because he was father's favorite.

Being father's favorite did not mean RJ had an easy life. Expectations were high for all father's children, especially RJ. Although we were provided for, none of us had a happy childhood, and after mother died life became even more demanding. RJ's sickliness became his armor against father; protection and a way to keep father at bay. RJ knew that any moan or groan would summon father into immediate submission. As a child and teenager this often meant an expensive purchase of some novelty item that caught RJ's attention. And father was quick to comply. Purchases and cash were easier to supply than genuine empathy, support or kindness. The price for these novelties was often more than RJ bargained for. Payback to father was often grueling and exhausting. These paybacks included some note-worthy task; a public appearance with father; an increased GPA; compensation for father's attention. The girls stopped seeking father's attention and were content achieving to please them-selves. RJ did not have that option. He was father's son and therefore he had standards to meet. These were never standards self administered but those established by father. Having father's attention was never fun and became less wanted as RJ grew up. It just meant the focus was on you to perform and always excel, or excel more! Father's image of what RJ grew into was far from who RJ really was. Not particularly talented at any one task RJ needed time and practice to accomplish the simplest of tasks. After realizing that his son was not very accomplished at anything father created a much more acceptable façade for his boy. RJ would be perfect and father would see to it.

Docile and complacent RJ obediently followed father's course of action. Having outgrown his sickliness RJ could no longer depend on that as an excuse. Although not particularly talented in any one area, RJ was kind and gentle and had a good heart. RJ dressed the way father wanted, spoke the way father spoke and shared thoughts as father would share thoughts. When not in father's company he was fun and playful and lov-ing to his sisters. Once we asked him how he could tolerate so much time with father and slyly RJ confined to us "lots of very expensive bourbon" we laughed and nothing more was said.

It wasn't till several years later; RJ was 30-years-old, still liv-ing with father, still under father's thumb, that we gathered for our youngest and last sister Alison's wedding. Weddings for the picture perfect fantasy family are ideal opportunities for Kodak moments to be saved and cherished for eternity. Our family portraits showed beautiful hair and flawless teeth but never a genuine emotion. Candid photos did not exist, probably because the pain would be too real to see. Flowers bloomed; cakes and table settings glittered, unaware of the years of pain and sorrow surrounding them. Everything would be beautiful. Father spared no expense when it came to his daughter's weddings. As is customary, Father was going to give our sister away even though we secretly joked he "had given all his girls away on the day of their births!"

RJ loved his sisters but had become more reclusive as he aged. RJ's life was limited, no family of his own, no known intimate relationship; only RJ and father living in our childhood home. Father's life long ambition was to be a doctor, but his family could not afford to send him to medical school. RJ was predestined to live out fathers dream but despite the best of efforts RJ could not pass the tests to get into medical school. Instead he was barely able to become a second-rate chiropractor. He often told us how he really wanted to teach elementary school but "it wasn't meant to be…"

The day of the wedding RJ was his usual quiet self, joking with his sisters yet staying out of the limelight. He sipped his bourbon while making sardonic references, to anyone who happened to be listening, about a long list of things "that were never meant to be" in his life. Everyone was hustling about not paying any attention to RJ. Without any fanfare RJ walked over to Alison, kissed her on the cheek, wished her a wonderful life and went to his room. Alison thought nothing of her brother's odd departure and stayed focused on the excitement of the moment. Hours went by and it was time for the wedding. There was no sign of RJ. Father went and knocked on RJ's door but there was no answer. Impatient to start on time father opened the door and saw RJ's neatly pressed suit hanging on the closet door and RJ's shoes which were shinned to perfection. Suddenly father realized he wasn't alone. RJ's lifeless body was hanging from the light fixture in the bathroom, a chair kicked out from below. Frantic to cut his son's body free, father screamed for assistance. We all appeared in RJ's room bewildered and shocked to see father lowering RJ's body to the floor. I held my sisters close as we all cried inconsolability. RJ's body now laid on the floor, father cradling the lifeless body in his arms, rocking and muttering over and over "my boy, my boy, my boy." The groomsmen, who had also heard the screams, were now present, trying to make sense out of the chaos. Alison's fiancée found an envelope containing a letter addressed to father next to an empty bottle of bourbon on RJ's dresser. Father continued rocking and cradling his son muttering "my boy, my boy, my boy". Alison cautiously approached their father asked coyly

"Father? Father? It's a note from RJ, What do you want us to do??"

"Read it." He muttered. "Just read it"

Alison began "Father, I can't do this anymore. I have tried to do everything you have wanted but I am a failure. As a child I was too sick to be the student or athlete you wanted. I hate my career and my business is a failure. I'm lonely and can't consume enough bourbon to fill the emptiness in my heart. I'm sorry father. I love you. RJ"

No one said a word. It felt like hours but it was only minutes until the medics arrived. Prying my brother's cold lifeless body out of our father's arms the medics asked if there was anyone who would stay with our father. Being the oldest and the least involved in the now defunct wedding I said I would. Alison and the bridal party went to tell her guests that there would not be a wedding that day, as I sat alone with father.

Refusing to get off the floor, father sat silently sobbing, holding the now tattered rope that had suspended my brother's dead body in the air. Father was unaware that I was even present, much the same as when RJ was alive. Clinging to the rope he muttered over and over "my boy, my boy, why? My boy" As I sat motionless. Father was never the same.

I didn't realize till many years later that it was an emotional void within my father that made him focus on perfection within each of his children. The three Radenhausen daughters and RJ were never really inadequate; the inadequacy was felt by our father and was projected on all his children. His solace was having a son. Father believed that he could fix himself thru his son. What father could not succeed at in his lifetime would be a success in RJ's. RJ was his second chance at life - a chance to get it perfect. Ironically, one hangmen's knot took both of them.

"God does for us what we can not do for ourselves"

Moment of Grace

*I*ronically, my last memory is my first memory. My life ended and began at the same moment when the car I was driving flew over the cement divider and landed tail-end forward on the freeway. All I remember is bright headlights, loud horns, and the final sound of tires screeching and breaking glass. And then, silence –

13 days later, I woke up in the area hospital. A steal rod in my left leg, a brace on my neck, a tube down my throat, pins in my left arm and more stitches than I could count. Most frightening of all was that I was alone. Just me and the machines that systematically pumped air and fluids thru me to keep me alive. Medical staff hurried around me, making sure that the machinery that was keeping me alive continued to do so. No family or friends around me as I listened to the attending medical professionals routinely check my vitals and review my situation, but I couldn't respond - my jaw was wired closed, my cheek bone shattered. I was aware that people were around me, but not anyone I knew. As quick as they came they were gone their work requiring their presence with the next mangled soul. This was to be my last of a series of self imposed accidents.

This accident proved to be too much for my family. Before this, my family always supported me. That is up until now.

From the time I was a teenager I loved danger. Whether jumping off cliffs into abandoned quarry holes or racing cars on the quarter mile stretch onto the thru way; It was a game. The greater the danger, the bigger the thrill. But I was no longer a teenager, I was an adult, alone and barely alive. My family had always been there for me and it felt strange not to have anyone with me now. My body was broken and my spirit damaged. My jaw was wired closed, my eyes were swelled shut, my nose and throat had tubes coming and going. Ironically, all I could do was listen. After I woke up hospital staff would casually chat in my direction about my condition as they checked my vitals and adjusted my limbs. I was still dependent on machines to keep me alive and I just laid there, listening and thinking, piecing together the remnants of my life. One doctor in particular, Dr. Horning, had a matter of fact attitude when he consulted on my case. Not one to mince words he was the first to discuss my blood test results from the time of the accident "Cocaine, Marijuana and Alcohol – lucky SOB to be alive" he murmured as he preformed the routine examination taking specific attention to the bruises and needle marks on my arms. "Too bad about the other car though…" My mind became confused – "another car? Did someone hit me?" I couldn't remember, I couldn't remember anything… After scribbling something into my chart Dr. Horning patted my leg and headed toward the door "ok Champ, rest up, I'll be back tomorrow" and away he went. "Another car?" I needed to know.

Days and Doctors came and went. My days were very much the same as the one before. I was getting stronger and now breathing on my own. Nothing more had been said to me about the other car and its role in the accident; that created mixed feelings for me. I had no memory of events leading to or during the accident and a fear inside me preferred to block everything out.

My family continued to distance themselves from me. Only my younger sister would send me an occasional get well card and finally, when I was able, I called her. Not familiar with the hospital phone number on her caller ID she picked up the call then hesitated as she heard my voice

"Hello? Kevin? Is that you? You really shouldn't call me…. I shouldn't be talking to you…"

"Casey yeah It's me, wait, don't hang up – I've missed you, why hasn't anyone visited or called me…" "Kevin I can't talk right now – its better if you just stay away, you know, after the accident and all…" "What are you talking about? I'm going to be fine.. I know everyone was pissed, I've screwed up a lot but that's over, I'm done being a screw-up…""Kevin, come on that's more than screwing up; they were our friends and neighbors; the baby was only 3-years-old and we told you not to drink…" "Casey I don't have any idea what you are talking about – This is Kevin, your brother… the one who has been in the hospital for the last 60 days!! How about showing a little sympathy for me!!" Casey exploded with anger "I CAN'T BELIEVE YOU - YOU destroyed this family you and your love of money and drugs. You refused to get help and refused to move out, you laughed at the law and your multiple arrests, you didn't care how Mom and Dad worried each time you left the house and each time you landed in the hospital or jail. You left behind a trail of broken promises and broken hearts. SYMPATHY for YOU??? What about the Whiteclause family? Do you have any sympathy for them?" Casey hung up the phone leaving me dismayed and distraught. I knew I needed to find out what happened that night. When the shift nurse came into my room I asked her what happened the night of my accident. She looked uncomfortable then suggested I speak to my family. I told her they were not talking to me and I needed to know. She said she would get Dr. Horning.

Dr. Horning happened to be on rounds in the hospital and responded immediately to the page.

As he entered he looked grim but in his matter of fact way he handed me a newspaper article with the headline "**Family of four die in head on collision, drunk driver to blame**"

I read no further, but Dr. Horning insisted. "Go on Champ, read the article," but I shook my head no. "Fine then, I'll give you the highlights, about time you hear the whole story" Dr.

Horning went on to tell me how I had been verbally fighting with my parents resisting their request for me to move out on my own. After all I was 22-years-old and they did not want to continue enabling my worthless lifestyle. I didn't have regular work, I did nothing to help the family I refused to become sober and I disrespected everything they worked for. I had been drinking most of that day and on that night we had had another verbal battle ending with me storming out, already intoxicated in search of more drugs. My truck had little to no gasoline so I snatched the keys to my father's car and away I went. Stopping for a six-pack and cigarettes I decided to get on the highway headed toward Detroit. Angry and disoriented I entered the highway at a very high speed only to now realize it was the exit ramp. The Whiteclause family was exiting the highway, on that exit ramp, headed home after their evening at the first local showing of the Lion King. They never knew what hit them. All I remember is bright headlights, loud horns, and the final sound of tires screeching and breaking glass..

It is now, ten years later and I am ten years sober. I never drank or drugged again after that night. My life did start anew, even while serving time for vehicular homicide. Sadly four people lost their lives because of my addiction and my repeated refusal to get help. I thought I knew it all. Now, I am physically crippled and slowly becoming emotionally whole. God must have a bigger plan in store for me, by sparing my life that awful night, the unmerited divine assistance I received. It's important that I be sober now and for whatever my future holds. I remember the Whiteclause family everyday and I honor them by staying sober. I never again want to be the cause of anyone's suffering because of my reckless behavior. I try to be an example of sobriety everyday. Such was my moment of grace.

Moonstruck Madness

*A*n apprehensive, but pleading voice beckoned to her companion "Pete??, Pete?, "

First there was no response, no movement not even the sound of breathing when suddenly a deep voice responded slowly from the bedroom.

"What the hell do you want??"

"It's almost noon and you aren't even awake yet, I thought we were going to do some sight seeing today, we're only in this port for 1 day and ..."

"I know I know, you want to do some site seeing" Pete mumbled in response.

Sheepishly grinning MaryAnn nodded, eager to roust Pete out of bed.

"Come on" she sweetly cajoled, "I never get to go anywhere and ..."

"I know I know, you want to do some site seeing". Reluctantly, Pete rolled himself to the side of the bed, dropped his legs off the side and sat upright. Thinking to himself "this was the dumbest thing I've ever done – I hate boats, I hate sight seeing - in fact I hate leaving home, The only thing that I'm remotely interested in is MaryAnn and right now I'm questioning that. My head throbs and I need a drink". A night on the town with the guys seemed like a great idea before heading out to sea; it just didn't feel so great now. Slowly rising to his feet, Pete scowled cantankerously at MaryAnn while meandering into the bathroom.

Aware of his foul mood but pleased that he was awake and moving about, MaryAnn contently began thumbing through tourist guide books. Although she had read these pamphlets a million times before, she happily immersed herself in the history and tradition of Kingston, and forgot all about Pete's foul mood. Kingston would be their first port of call and her first experience abroad. MaryAnn had never been on a cruise before, in fact, she had never been out of the United States. Knowing Pete would never initiate a trip like this she had made all the arraignments. Although every bit of the trip was pre-approved by Pete, it was very evident that she was the more excited of the two. MaryAnn had counted down the days, months in advance, anticipating what might be a once in a lifetime excursion.

Trying not to appear impatient MaryAnn waited as Pete showered and shaved. Appearing overwhelmed with the simple task of choosing what to wear Pete retreated to his place in bed. Not saying a word, MaryAnn looked totally frustrated as Pete snapped

"Don't look at me like that"

"I didn't say a word"

"Yeah but I don't like that look – just give me a couple minutes to think so stop pushing me, I told you we would go sight seeing and we will" as he clicked on the remote for the television. MaryAnn looked away to hide her disappointment when suddenly Pete spoke up using a much kinder tone

"Hey Hon? How about going out to the bar and bringing back a couple cold ones - See if they have Heineken? If not try to find something else imported..." his voice faded away as his attention now focused on the television. MaryAnn said nothing but left the cabin and proceeded to find the bar. Thinking to herself "the sooner he is comfortable the sooner he'll be ready to go out" undaunted, she continued her search. Successfully finding the bar and retrieving the beer she returned to the cabin. With beer in hand, MaryAnn entered the cabin surprised to find Pete, dressed, groomed and ready to go out.

"You didn't think I would disappoint my best girl, now would you? Let's go and see what Jamaica is all about!!" MaryAnn tossed the beer aside and threw her arms around Pete's neck.

"I love you, Pete" "I love you too honey"

And out they went.

Pete and MaryAnn made a striking couple. Dressed in native garb they hardly looked like tourists. Their tanned skin covered by the loose light colored cotton short sleeved shirts, khaki shorts, and sandals. Pete was tall and burley, his physic well defined in the tropical sun. His head of thick brown hair had a natural wave women swooned for. His gait was confident and masterful as if he ruled whatever turf he strode. MaryAnn was trim and neat, of average height and adequate build. Her brown hair tied back in a loose ponytail with simple gold earrings caught the mid day sun. Both had easy effortless smiles that put everyone instantly at ease. It was MaryAnn's soft spoken, gentle manner that first caught Pete's attention and eventually his heart. Pete was not an easy man to love. He was prone to excess; Pete worked hard, played hard, partied hard. Having come from essentially nothing Pete was a self made man and was proud of it. Having his own construction business by the age of twenty-five he was quite proud and protective of his accomplishments. Social opportunities were networking opportunities and Pete was game for both. Pete could charm a rattle snake or be the rattle snake depending on his mood. And his mood could change in an instant.

MaryAnn could hardly contain her excitement as they exited the ship. Skipping down the gang way she was rattling bits of information she had read earlier, comparing it to what she was actually seeing now and what she anticipated seeing later. The dock was packed full of eager tourists, some looking for their tour groups, some looking for family members and other just trying to get their bearings. Pete hated crowds and wanted to move thru as fast as possible. Grabbing MaryAnn's wrist he pushed thru the dawdling masses and maneuvered around the crowd to an area off the dock. The rhythm of steal drums and calypso music could be heard in the distance enticing the couple to come closer. MaryAnn, eager to tour the island, resisted the tempting draw of the music, and continued moving toward the tour group but Pete was equally tempted by the joviality of the music and guided her in its direction. The music was coming from a beach bar.

Once it was within Pete's sight he moved even faster in its direction.

"Come on Honey, Let's sit down and have a drink" Pete had already scoped out two empty seats at the bar and was practically sprinting toward them, clutching MaryAnn's wrist and dragging her in tow. " "

Resigned to Pete's will, she murmured "I guess... but just one, I really want to see the island..." Pete smiled and nodded approvingly, pleased to have his way as the pair settled in at the bar. Pete's loud voice commanded the attention of the bartender

"What kind of wine do you have?"

"Red, white and white zinfandel"

"That's it? Give the lady a glass of your white zinfandel and a glass of white wine for me - make sure I get a full glass, not just a taste!"

The bartender served the wine without embellishment. Pete bristled as he noted only ¾ of the glass was filled. "Is this the best you can do? I wanted a full glass!"

The bartender continued serving customers as he responded unemotionally

"That's a glass of wine, take it or leave it"

Pete, angered at the indifference of the bartender, stood and attempted to face off with him. Only the teak bar and MaryAnn, were between Pete and the bartender. Pete was now focused on the seemingly insubordinate bartender. Primed for a fight, Pete prepared to pounce on the unassuming bartender as MaryAnn pleaded "PETE, (hesitation) Sit Down, (more hesitation) please-let's not do this here, remember we're on vacation, PLEASE?" Pete, sat down, grumbled a final insult at the bartender, who appeared oblivious to the whole encounter, and proceeded to take a long lingering taste of his wine. As he savored the wine instantly his demeanor became calm. The music of the calypso and the cool ocean breeze helped restore the peacefulness that only moments earlier had been disturbed by Pete's explosive temper. With peace being restored, MaryAnn exhaled a long sigh of relief, but tense from the near altercation.

"ahhh, come on honey, relax", beseeched Pete as he sipped a long sip of wine "this is our vacation". Not sure if Pete was being serious or sarcastic MaryAnn sat back and tried to relax. In a loud, demanding voice Pete ordered a round of drinks for the lingering patrons as he settled in. Still trying to appear relaxed, MaryAnn sipped her white zinfandel and made small talk with other patrons. She anxiously waited. And waited, and waited. Pete, ignored her longing glances as he became more comfortable where he was sitting and with what he was drinking. He had no plans to leave any time soon.

Sipping his wine, Pete made an unexpected attempt at being charming as he leaned into MaryAnn and inquired.

"Honey? How about another glass of Zinfandel? Pete, knowing MaryAnn was not one to sit and just drink had hoped she might consume more than a single drink. MaryAnn looked away, irritated that her first day on a tropical island was being spent in a bar, and even more irritated that Pete was ok with it. Ironically MaryAnn was not surprised; many an evening turned out to be less than stellar when Pete started to drink. But being an optimist MaryAnn always hoped that perhaps the next outing would be different, and really wanted this cruise to be special. She had been dating Pete off and on for a couple years and she was ready to settle down and start a family. As much as she loved Pete she had her doubts that he could be the kind of family man she wanted. She was hoping this cruise would give her clarity.

Sweetly Pete beseeched her "Come on hon, just one more drink, I'm just starting to unwind..."

"No, No thanks, I don't want anything to drink. Pete? Can we go soon? I really want to see the island and...

"What the hell is the matter with you?" Pete blasted at MaryAnn.

"Can't you relax for 5 minutes? Do we have to be moving all the time? Get off my back... Damn it to hell woman this is MY vacation too...If you want to sight see then go, but I'm staying here!" Gulping down the wine that was left in his glass, he ordered another drink and turned his back to MaryAnn. MaryAnn said nothing. Feeling alone and foolish as several patrons were now looking in her direction MaryAnn went to the ladies room to recompose herself. Fixing her now tear smeared makeup, MaryAnn prepared herself to rejoin Pete at the bar. Thinking to her self, "maybe if I don't pester him he'll finish his drink and we'll still be able to do some sight seeing". Undaunted and very optimistic, MaryAnn left the ladies room to join Pete.

Resuming her place next to Pete, MaryAnn, confidently signaled the bartender and she ordered lemonade. Pete, noticing her non-alcoholic drink choice, snickered and continued his conversation with the ever changing patrons. MaryAnn noticed that the more Pete drank the louder and more opinionated he became. He also took less and less notice of her and more and more notice of every other woman who came into the bar. MaryAnn said nothing, but sat with her lemonade, resigned to wait for Pete to finish.

Afternoon gradually turned into evening. The sun was gently setting and the tourists who had been on tours throughout the day were working their way back to the ship. Some were stopping at the beach bar for a drink before re-boarding the ship. MaryAnn, perched on her stool next to Pete, looked enviously at the other tourists who carried their bags filled with their new baubles. She listened to their stories and wished it had been her venturing on this tropical island. Instead, she had sat in the very familiar surroundings of a bar, with Pete, the entire day.

Tired from doing nothing and very aware that she was the only sober person at the beach bar, MaryAnn suggested to Pete that they too return to the ship. The arrival of new faces at the bar seemed to rejuvenate Pete and he now basked in the attention of the ship-bound tourists. Pete agreed, it was time to return to the ship but only if his new found entourage would join him for one more drink at the ships bar. MaryAnn, resigned to a lost day, with no fight left in her, returned to the ship with Pete and company.

The ships' bar was packed as Pete, MaryAnn and his merry group arrived. Pete loved a full bar and he was in his glory. Barely aware of MaryAnn, Pete ordered a round of drinks for everyone, then noticing MaryAnn he sarcastically added "and get my girl anything but lemonade, she's sour enough!!" Laughing at his joke and repeating it as if to make it funnier, Pete laughed uncontrollably. Having been drinking all day, Pete was far more inebriated than any of the other patrons. MaryAnn had had enough, enough lemonade, enough barroom conversation, enough of Pete. Politely excusing herself, she bid goodnight to the patrons who were seated close to her. MaryAnn left the bar and returned to her cabin, without Pete. Climbing into bed alone MaryAnn reassured herself that" Pete would be in any time now – he was probably on his way to the cabin and would be in bed before she fell asleep". Restlessly waiting for Pete, MaryAnn finally drifted off to sleep, unaware of where Pete was, but optimistic he would return to their cabin soon. She couldn't have been more wrong.

A half hour went by before Pete noticed that MaryAnn was gone but it made no difference to him. The bar had started to clear out as patrons were returning to their cabins, preparing for the next day at sea. Pete had no intention of turning in for the night as he became engrossed in a flirtatious exchange with an attractive brunette who had taken the stool previously occupied by MaryAnn. Pete was mesmerized by this new attractive creature. Pete watched the way she held her glass in one hand, a cigarette in the other and systematically inhaled her cigarette and drink with equal finesse. Her perfume had a soft sweet smell only salient to those close at hand. Leaning close to her he deviously asked "We've been talking for an hour and we don't even know each others names – I'm Pete."

"I'm Natalie, pleasures mine"

"We'll see about that, what the hell are you drinking, Ms. Natalie? I'd like to buy you… a drink that is…"

"A cosmopolitan," she replied as she spun her stool closer to his. "I hate drinking alone, don't you?"

"Nawh, it depends on the company, I'd rather drink alone than with poor company, but with good company I could drink all night long!"

Gazing directly at Pete, Natalie responded coquettishly, "Really? All night?" Pete grinned back at her, put his arm around the back of her stool, and ordered them both another drink. Once again leaning close to Natalie, Pete inhaled the aroma of her perfume

"What is that delicious smell?" Pete asked as he seemed to be drawn closer to the smell

"Moonstruck Madness, delicious isn't it? " Natalie replied with a silly laugh which further intrigued Pete

"hummm Moonstruck Madness ? That I am my dear, that I am…" as he ordered another round

"To new found friends" Pete whispered to Natalie as she raised her glass to his toast and with equal finesse Pete leaned over and kissed her cheek

Gazing back at Pete, Natalie responded "Yes, to new friends…" Pete threw back his drink and signaled the bartender for another round.

MaryAnn woke up at 3:00 am alarmed that Pete was not in bed. Debating whether to search the ship bars to see if he was still drinking or passed out somewhere on deck, she considered waiting until morning to look for him. Suddenly fearful that he may have fallen overboard MaryAnn considered calling the concierge to look for him. After another half hour she made the call.

"Hello? This is MaryAnn Uhler in cabin 5050 my companion, Pete Styles, did not return to our cabin and I was hoping you may have seen him somewhere on the ship? He was drinking a lot and may have forgotten where our cabin is…"

"Yes mamm' m we can check the bars and decks to see if he is lost." "I would appreciate that, He's a tall man, clean shaven and quite muscular with dark eyes and dark hair …I would really appreciate if you could look for him… Thank-you"

"yes mamm, good night"

"Good night" feeling somewhat more relieved MaryAnn went back to sleep, once again confident that Pete would return soon.

Waking up several hours later MaryAnn woke up in a panic. Pete was not in bed; in fact he wasn't in the cabin. There was no sign that he had returned to the cabin at all that night. Immediately fearing the worst MaryAnn believed that something awful must have happened to Pete. Thinking to her self she imagined several possibilities "Maybe he did fall over board, Maybe he fell and hit his head and is in a coma bleeding somewhere on the boat or maybe he got into a fight with someone and is laying somewhere unconscious and hurt..." scrambling to get dressed MaryAnn threw on shorts and a tee shirt and bolted out of the cabin "If something happened to him I'll never forgive myself" and out she went resolved to find Pete.

Unbeknownst to MaryAnn, Pete was quite fine. Sleeping soundly in a luxury cabin on the top deck Pete woke to the sound of the ocean tossing against the ship. Momentarily waking and thinking to himself "Where the hell am I?" he rolled over and fell back to sleep. Hours went by as Pete lay passed out next to Natalie, too hung over to consider getting up; too drunk to care. By afternoon the bed had stopped spinning and Pete was able to sit up. Observing the remnants from last night's partying Pete set his sights on retrieving an unidentified, abandoned mixed drink that was almost within his reach at the far side of his night stand; the muddled fruit, diluted with what was at one time ice and decorated with a bedraggled paper umbrella seemed to call to him. Rolling to one side and stretching as far as he could, his fingers barely touched the side of the glass. Finally Pete was able to nudge the glass into his hand. Thinking "Ah Success" he chugged the watered down fruit infused alcohol then proceeded to collect his clothing and get dressed. Once assembled, he tossed a blanket over Natalie's naked sleeping body, and exited her cabin. "Time for a drink" he thought as he entered the hallway and undaunted he went in search of the closest bar.

By afternoon MaryAnn was exhausted and exasperated. She had walked the entire ship with no success in finding Pete. Finally returning to their cabin she had hoped he might be in their bed waiting for her and this was all a terrible dream. She opened the door, looked to the bed and realized this was not a dream. Pete was missing. She would have to report this to the ship's captain.

Briefly pausing to wash up, brush her hair and quickly freshening her make-up MaryAnn opened the cabin door to make one last search for Pete before reporting him missing. As she turned the door knob she could feel someone on the other side also turning the knob. Opening the door was Pete. So grateful to see him MaryAnn threw her arms around his neck and exclaimed "You had me so worried! I thought you fell over board – I didn't know what to think, I was sooo scared! I couldn't stand it if anything happened to you. Ahhh, Pete, why would you scare me like that?" Pete sheepishly broke free from MaryAnn's grasp and flopped on the bed, face down. Sweetly and cautiously MaryAnn asked "Pete? What's going on? Where have you been??" She had noticed that Pete smelt like stale cigarette smoke and alcohol and maybe a faint scent of something sweet, like roses. Pete rolled on his side, as not to look at MaryAnn and stated defiantly "Don't start lecturing me, can't you see I'm tired? I didn't come back here to listen to your shit. Why don't you go on one of those tours you were so interested in yesterday? Just go away..." MaryAnn looked stunned, thinking to herself "doesn't he realize that I was the one that was worried; I was the one scanning the ship looking for him. Why was HE yelling at ME???" MaryAnn had been with Pete long enough to recognize the stages of his drunkenness. Right now he was VERY drunk which meant he could be VERY nasty. Normally, she would just stay away from him until he sobered up. Once he was sober he would become remorseful, and eventually apologized. It's just how he was. Today was different; it felt different to MaryAnn. She decided she wasn't going to go away; at least not until she had some answers. And she was willing to wait.

No amount of coaxing or cajoling could move Pete when he was this drunk, so Maryann sat on the bed next to him. Yes, she would wait. Watching this man sleep made her think of a gentle giant. He looked so peaceful and calm. Not like the raging drunk that cared for no one but himself. Gently rubbing his back, MaryAnn could feel his muscles relax and yield to her touch. Feeling his body loosen up she snuggled her head in the nap of his neck and she began to tenderly kiss him as the faint smell of bitter roses became stronger and very apparent to her. It was perfume. Pulling away in shock MaryAnn allowed herself one more breath of the sweet but pungent aroma permeating Pete's perimeter. Yes, it was women's perfume, and not MaryAnn's. She had her answer.

While Pete slept, MaryAnn stealthily packed her bag and left. She left Pete, the cabin and the ship. She flew a commercial flight back to the states and was able to move away from Pete before the cruise finally docked. She made sure she would never see him again.

Pete's drinking caused chaos in MaryAnn's life and she had had enough. It was more than a spoiled vacation. It was the humiliation and degradation she felt knowing he didn't respect or care about her when he was drunk. And he was drunk most of the time. Alcohol mattered more than anything to Pete and no woman would ever matter as much. MaryAnn felt like an ass, first for trusting him, secondly for tolerating his endless need to drink, and lastly for accepting his bad behavior. MaryAnn knew she deserved better and knowing that made her feel better.

Life can either be accepted or changed.
If it is not accepted, it must be changed.
If it cannot be changed, then it must be accepted.

—Winston Churchill.

Addict in the Attic

Everything about Allison was normal. She came from a normal family and had normal friends, who did normal things. She went to regular schools and had normal grades. There was nothing unusual about Allison. Allison was a late life baby, conceived when mother and father were no longer concerned with the need for birth control. Father died before Alison's 5th birthday leaving mother to raise Allison alone. Mother bent over backwards trying to over compensate for the lack of paternal parenting. There were 19-years between us and although we had the same parents we were not raised the same. I had left home soon after Allison was born and in a lot of ways she was a stranger to me. Allison and I were never close

As was our routine, my husband Jonathan, and I would stop by my mother's house on Saturdays to visit with her. Sometimes we would bring lunch or just have a cup of coffee. Allison, was seldom home, always busy with friends or other activities. This particular Saturday was different as Mother was waiting on the porch as we walked up the sidewalk to her house. "shushhhhhhhhhhh – Allison is sleeping" mother warned as we stepped onto the porch. "She worked late last night and needs her rest". Unaccustomed to the silent vigil on a Saturday afternoon Jonathan and I stealthily entered mother's house. As was the routine we had completed our weekly errands and were stopping to visit with mother. This was the first week Allison had worked since graduating from college and mother was euphoric. It had been two years since Allison graduated and Mother had been the one to cover Allison's debts since Allison had not found suitable employment. Mother did not want anything to interfere with this employment opportunity.

While growing up Allison had the best of everything; first the best toys, then the best clothes, phones, computers, cars, schools and on and on. Mother often worked two jobs to provide for all of Allison's trinkets. It was as if mother thought she could compensate for Allison's lack of fathering by giving her whatever she wanted. Allison was demanding and learned to expect the best. And mother learned to provide.

Mother was now almost 68-years-old and longed for full time retirement. Always fearful that Allison's lack of ambition would hinder mother's retirement, we had hoped that acquiring this job might be the first step toward Allison, and mother's, emancipation.

Heeding mother's warning, Jonathan and I tip-toed into the kitchen and sat down. Mother sat down too but she seemed uncomfortable.

"So what kind of work is Allison doing? I asked, mostly to be polite.

"Oh, it's a wonderful job, she gets dressed up every day, and she has a fancy phone and her own secretary... It's truly a wonderful job"

"But what does she do?" I asked again

"It's a wonderful job" mother repeated and then became abrupt "I don't want you pressuring your sister for details and making her angry..." Mother was always hyper protective of Allison so I dropped the subject.

Making small talk usually suited mother well but today was different, and she seemed anxious and almost eager for us to leave. Sensing her fretfulness we said our good bys. I shrugged off Mother's odd behavior as her age or maybe the change in schedule because of Allison working.   We left the house and continued with our errands not giving the visit another thought.

The next week we arrived in our usual fashion to visit with mother. It was Saturday and we were a little earlier than usual. As we stepped onto the porch we could hear loud voices coming from inside the house. Instantly concerned, we entered thru the door that lead into the kitchen where the voices were clearer. It was mother and Allison. Allison, still wearing her pajama bottoms, and a faded tee-shirt; her unkempt hair loosely tied in a pony tail swishing from side to side. Shoeless she stood in an aggressive stance as one hand held mother's wrist and the other was poised to strike. Mother looked small and frail compared to Allison and very helpless.

"What's going on here? Mom? You ok? Allison? What the hell are you doing? I shouted as I entered the room, Jonathan in tow. My voice began to quiver as I realized what was happening.

"Allison? Let go of her! Answer me". Allison, stunned to see us and in an apparent rage, released mother's wrist as she stormed out of the room and stomped up the stairs to her room in the attic. I turned my attention to my mother

"Mom? Tell me what's going on." I asked besiegingly. She just shook her head and rubbed her wrist. Reluctantly she murmured

"Nothing, nothing at all. Your sister and I were having a disagreement. Nothing serious..." Mother's tone changed as she launched her attack on me

"You should knock before you go barging into someone's house" "I raised you better than that!" she snarled.

Dumbstruck, I looked to Jonathan to confirm what I just heard and what we both had seen. Jonathan started to speak but before a word came out mother had changed the subject.

"Jonathan? Would you mind helping me get the groceries out of the car?" "Allison needs her sleep and I shouldn't have tried to wake her, she's just cranky, you know how she gets, I shouldn't have bothered her - now, I don't want you talking about Allison anymore, she's trying so hard and has so much stress."

"Sure, no problem, I'll get the groceries," as he threw a quisling look in my direction he headed toward the door and hesitated. Then mother focused on me, and her tone changed but yet again, becoming kind and gracious.

"Sweetie ? Would you balance my check book? You know I'm not good with numbers"

"Sure Mom, where is it?" Now you know where I keep it, it's in the top drawer of the desk"

Jonathan obligingly went about retrieving the groceries as I went to balance Mother's checkbook.

"Mom? It's not here – I can't find the checkbook... Are you sure you left it here?

"Of course I did, I always put it in the same place... It has to be .. here..." her voice trailed off and in an unusual false forced voice mother appeared to change her mind about the checkbook.

"Know what? I ran out of checks and must have left my checkbook on the counter at the bank when I was ordering more checks; I'll call the bank in the morning I'm sure it's there..."

"Mom? Why would you leave your checkbook anywhere! That's not like you..."

"Please stop questioning me! You are wearing me out with all these questions"

By this time Jonathan returned after unloading the groceries. "You ready to go?" he asked me sensing the tension between me and my mother.

"Yes, I'm ready. You sure you're ok Mom? Should I say something to Allison?"

"No NO, no, just let Allison sleep. She'll be fine, she just needs to sleep"

We said our goodbyes and got into our car.

"That was the most ridiculous thing I've ever seen" Jonathan stated as he started the car.

"Do you think Allison was going to hurt Mom?" I asked him knowing he was not one to feed into drama.

"It sure looked that way, but your mom seems to have it under control. After all she certainly wasn't looking for our help..."

"It sure was strange" We road home in silence as nothing more was said about the strange encounter at mom's house.

Later that evening, both Jonathan and I were still feeling uncomfortable with the events we witnessed earlier in the day at mom's house. We didn't say much to each other but neither of us thought about much else. Finally Jonathan suggested we go check on mom and I jumped at the opportunity. Within seconds we were back in the car and on our way to my mother's house.

When we pulled in front of the house I noticed that the house was unusually dark. Mom's car was parked in its usual spot so it was easy to assume she'd be home. Mom had got into the habit of turning her porch light on at dusk and it was well after dusk, and there was no light on. Her front room and kitchen looked dark as well. I became anxious and got out of the car and quickly ran toward the house. The kitchen door was unlocked and slightly ajar. The kitchen was dark

"Mom?? Mom? Where are you?" "Jonathan? Something's wrong" frantically I moved through the kitchen into her sitting room and there was mom, sitting in the dark holding a package of frozen peas against her face. "Oh ma, what happened?" Jonathan sat next to her, gently removing the bag of frozen peas and examining her face. "Where's Allison? I began to shout, "Why isn't she here?" "Your sister left; I don't know where she went" mother mumbled as her head dropped forward and her eyes rolled back; that quickly mom was unconscious. Jonathan quickly grabbed his cell phone and called for an ambulance. Within minutes one appeared and was taking mom to the hospital. After locking mom's door and securing the house, we too

125

embarked to the hospital. Not saying a word we knew what the other was thinking, "where was Allison?" Our ride to the hospital was quite and even though it was only a short distance, it seemed to take forever. Once we arrived at the hospital the medics swiftly moved mother from the ambulance into the emergency room. Doctors and admission people were trying to extract the minimum information we had to offer. Everything seemed very chaotic as people were moving quickly to and fro with apparent purpose. As I looked up through the crowd of people my eyes met with Allison. She was by herself across the room – her eyes were dark and sunken – her face was grey and pasty looking. She looked like a walking corpse. I raised my hand to motion her to join me but she was gone. Frantic to find her I dropped the papers I was signing and ran toward the door closest to where Allison had been standing. She was gone. Suddenly someone was yelling my name and I momentarily forgot about Allison. It was Jonathan, walking toward me "I just talked to the doctor and he says your mom will be ok, she has a concussion and bruised ribs but she'll be ok". Relieved, I thanked God she was ok as Jonathan continued "one more thing, she can't stay by herself" he paused, "I told the hospital to release her to us since we haven't spoke to Allison" I threw my arms around him and I started to cry, realizing someone had caused mother's injuries and I didn't want to believe it may have been because of Allison. "Allison". I sobbed "Oh Jonathan, I saw her, she was in the emergency room, she looked awful but she left before I could get to her.

"Let's take care of your mother, get her home and settled in and then we'll worry about Allison" Jonathan was so sensible and practical. I appreciated his kindness toward Mother and his objectiveness toward Allison. I was less optimistic.

As we drove home we passed mother's house. The house was dark except for a dim light shinning through the sky light in the attic. "Allison must be home" I whispered to Jonathan who nodded in acknowledgement, not wanting to distress mother. We continued home in silence. No one slept well that night. Mother was restless from her injuries, Jonathan was uncomfortable after the day's events and I was full of anxiety and questions. I could not understand what my younger sister's role was in mother's trauma.

As the days and weeks went by mother became stronger and was able to be more independent. She continued living with us never asking to return to her house. We had not heard from Allison and no one ever brought up her name. Occasionally I would drive by mother's house and I would see the single light on in the attic, shinning through the skylight in Allison's room. I knew, at the very least Allison was home then. Not wanting to upset mother I choose to believe that Allison was working long hours, caring for mother's house and getting her life organized. Secretly we each wondered why Allison didn't call, not even once. The better Mother felt the more she started to talk about returning to her house. Realistically, it was time. It had been six weeks since mother's accident. Mother's doctor had released her from his care and she talked more and more frequently about her plants, her garden and her life, in her home. We decided Saturday would be a good day to take Mother home. Jonathan and I decided to call Allison and tell her our plan.

Numerous attempts to reach Allison were not successful. Her cell phone was often turned off and when it was on the mailbox was full. Calls to her supposed employer were just as frustrating as the only response we were given was that no one with that name was employed by them. Frustrated and unsure of what was happening at mother's house we decided to stop by, without mother, and take a look for ourselves before moving her back in. Nothing could have prepared us for what we found. As we approached the house everything seemed pretty much as we last saw it – the grass was over grown, shrubs could use a trim, but other than that it appeared fine. As we walked on to the porch it was obvious all the shades had been drawn and the screen door looked like it had been kicked in, as it now was hanging from one hinge; the screen no longer intact. I turned the door knob and the door was not locked. It opened easily. Jonathan entered first and I stayed close behind him.

The kitchen was unkempt; the garbage was overflowing, the sink was piled high with unwashed dishes and my shoes stuck to the floor in places where something had spilt and was never wiped up. All of the shades we pulled down and the curtains were closed tightly so no one could see in or see out. In some windows extra cover was placed over the whole window making it impossible for light to show through. As we walked through the living room it felt oddly orderly. Newspapers were stacked in one direction in a neat pile, magazines were equally as neat. The throw rugs which Mother placed in no special order were now all lined up, their pattern matching the one next to it. Mother's collection of ceramic animals were lined up from tallest to smallest all facing east. The final touch was seeing Mother's DVD collection, which filled the television stand and never had a specific order was now in alphabetical order!

I exclaimed "Now I've seen everything!! Something is really wrong" Jonathan was too shocked to reply but kept moving through the house. We had gone through the whole house with no sight of Allison. We approached the stairs that lead to the attic, and Allison's room. Light was coming from her room casting a eerie glow upon the stairs as Jonathan and I cautiously and slowly ascended to her room. The ceiling was angled, following the construction of the roof line changing with the peeks of the roof. Somewhat lower than a traditional ceiling the angels gave a cozy, cabin-like feeling to the room. Just like downstairs all the windows were covered allowing the only light to come and go through a skylight. Huddled in a corner was Allison. A blanket wrapped around her now small frame didn't move, even after we called her name. I feared she was dead. "Allison!! Allison can you hear me! Why won't you answer??" Slowly Allison poked her head out from under the blanket. Her cheekbones were very pronounced, her eyes dark and sunken, and many open sores appeared on her face. Suddenly she became anxious and aggressive as she started screaming

"What do you want? Get out of my room, BOTH of you GET OUT now, GET OUT NOW! Who is with you? I know that there are others with you... did you bring the police? Shit, ARE THEY IN MY HOUSE? All OF YOU GET OUT!!

"Allison, no one is with us, Allison it's just your sister and me" Jonathan tried to reason with her using his most calming voice, trying to make eye contact with her, but with no success. Allison looked like a cornered wild animal, ready to strike at any second. Springing to her feet, clinging to her blanket, she frantically paced from one side of the room to the other, intermittently stopping at the window and cautiously moving the shade and peering out as if expecting to be invaded.

"We're not going to hurt you; we want to help you..." Jonathan besieged. Looking in my direction he mouthed "call 911". Allison was now standing still; the blanket was draped on her shoulders like a cape. She stood in the same aggressive stance she had when she fought with Mother so many weeks earlier. Frantically, Allison began scratching her arms, and began ranting about bugs crawling on her skin. I looked to Jonathan who also looked bewildered – neither of us saw any bugs. Fortunately, within minutes the medics once again arrived at my mother's house, this time to get Allison. Still wrapped in a blanket Allison became combative, trying to battle the medics, Jonathan and me. Swinging wildly her fist landed squarely across the nose of one medic, as he backed off in obvious pain, Jonathan and the remaining medic were able to grab and hold Allison down. Finally in restraints, Allison was loaded into the ambulance with Jonathan and me in tow. Before we left I turned out all the lights in mother's house. This time it was truly dark.

We arrived at the hospital as Allison was being carried into the emergency ward. The medics had given her a sedative to calm her down and it was working. Allison had stopped trying to fight and now appeared to be sleeping. We waited impatiently for the doctor to finish examining her. It seemed to take forever. Finally, the doctor came out to talk to us. He said his name was Dr. Goodman and he would be Allison's attending physician. He continued to explain that Allison was addicted to Methamphetamine and immediately we assumed the doctor had to be wrong as I felt compelled to defend my little sister. "Allison was a good girl, sure she could be rebellious and God knows she's spoiled but not a Meth... addict... Wasn't that a bikers drug? Not a college kids drug... "The doctor explained how Meth was being used in many rural and suburban areas and he continued "Because it's such a highly addictive drug, using meth a few times can lead to getting hooked" Jonathan and I nodded in agreement, It hadn't been that long since Allison's personality started to change — and we were seeing the effects of this drug which are ugly and scary. Dr. Goodman continued "It can make you lose weight, lose your teeth and develop scabs and open sores on your skin and face. Chronic meth abusers can become anxious and violent." Now it was making sense. Allison had shown signs of using Meth when she became violent with Mother. It all became clear; her neurotic obsessive cleaning and unpredictable bursts of energy, then crashing and sleeping only to wake up angry and agitated, her paranoia and delusions that people were watching her. Yes it now made sense.

"So what can we do? " I asked the doctor.

"You have several options, you could take her home but chances are she will continue using Meth, regardless of what she may say or promise you. Meth is powerfully addictive and powerfully damaging to your body and brain". Dr. Goodman continued "You could see if she is willing to go into inpatient treatment and stop using Meth all together."

"Are there any other choices?" I asked sheepishly.

"I'm afraid not, why don't you go home and think about it and we'll talk about it in the morning. Allison needs to spend the night here regardless."

"That sounds like good advice, let's go home and sleep on it "Jonathan chimed in. He was tired and ready to go home anyway.

"Can I see her before we leave" I asked the doctor

"She's still sedated and sleeping but of course you can see her" "We'll talk tomorrow, get some rest." He kindly pat my shoulder and shook Jonathan's hand before he walked away.

Holding Jonathan's hand I entered Allison's room. Allison looked grey, almost bluish as she lay sleeping. An IV line attached to a glucose solution, and blood pressure cuff attached to her arm, I could hear the methodic humming and beeping of the monitors creating a peaceful serene rhythm as we entered the room. Allison didn't move as I sat down beside her. Looking at her I couldn't believe that my baby sister was a Meth addict. Holding her hand I could see how thin and gaunt her arms were, she looked almost malnourished like someone from a third world nation. Looking at her arms I couldn't help but see the open sores and scabs which she had picked to the point of oozing. Her face was speckled with more open sores that she had recently picked open. I recalled her screaming that bugs were crawling on her, when nothing was there; "Guess that explains all the talk about bugs" Jonathan nodded, silently acknowledging what we now know were Allison's hallucinations. We sat with Allison and said nothing as the machines attached to her pumped life into her limp body.

The next day we woke up early, eager to call the hospital for an update on Allison. Fortunately mother was sound asleep when we got home from the hospital but now we would have to tell her about her youngest daughter. Jonathan and I had hardly slept all night. When I did sleep, I had disturbing dreams about drugs, death and my sister. I wanted this to be over. I wanted to wake up and this all be a bad dream. I wanted my mother and sister to be living happily across town. I wanted Saturday afternoon visits and light conversations. I wanted our family to be normal. I was afraid angry, and bitter with Allison for doing this to us. And now we would have to tell mother.

Mother was cheerfully attending to her morning routine when we joined her in the kitchen.

"Mom? Jonathan and I need to talk to you. It's kind of important"

"Sure hon, just let me finish folding these towels and then we can talk" putting the towels away she sat down and innocently looked to me to start the conversation, I sat next to Mother and took her hand, more for my reassurance and comfort than hers.

"Mom, I don't know how else to say this so I'm going to get right to the point. Allison has been abusing a substance known as Methamphetamine and she's addicted to it" there, I said it. I took a deep breath and I sighed, relieved that I said it aloud. I looked to Jonathan for support and back to Mother to see how she processed the information. Mother's expression did not change, in fact she was so non-responsive I feared she didn't even hear me.

"Mom? I said Allison is a drug addict – that's why she's been acting odd, it was the drugs making her become angry and violent... Mom?"

"I heard you" mother responded in a cold distant tone. "Why would you say such awful things about your baby sister? I can't believe that you would be so mean as to call her a drug addict"

Stunned and speechless I let Jonathan continue "Mom, it's true, Allison has been using Methamphetamine to give her energy and slow her appetite. It's not a good drug or even a drug doctor's can prescribe. It's made in illegal labs with mixtures of cleaning fluids, battery acid and over the counter cold medications - God only knows what else can end up in it, Regardless, without professional treatment, Allison could die." Jonathan's voice sounded firm and final.

"Allison has been under a lot of stress..." I interrupted, irritated at her defense of Allison

"No Mom, Allison has been using illegal drugs that have caused her to be stressed" I could feel my face flush with color as my voice was getting louder and louder.

"Allison hurt you while she was under the influence of Meth, she lost her job and she may loose her life if we don't do something now!" I could not believe that Mother was still in denial even after being a witness to Allison's bizarre and unpredictable behaviors and a victim of her rage.

"The doctor suggests that Allison go into an inpatient addictions treatment facility as soon as she can breathe on her own and is able to travel..." Mother shook her head defiantly.

"There is NO way I am putting my child away with drug addicts. She is NOT a drug addict! This is a mistake. Someone must have tricked her or put something in her drink. NOT MY CHILD! If anyone is going to be there for her it will be me! I WILL help her, I'm her mother, and I'm the one she needs, not strangers and not a rehab!" Jonathan sat next to Mother and gently took her hand in his

"Mom, I know this isn't what you wanted to hear and we are just as upset as you are, but Allison needs more help, trained professional help, if she is going to get away from using the Meth."

"We are a good family and she is a good girl and I know she is not using drugs!" mother wailed... "I will care for your sister and that's all that's to it. I don't want you saying ANYTHING about this to ANYONE. Humphhhhh; drug addict; I've never heard anything so ridiculous!" Mother scowled and shook her hand free from Jonathan's as I opened my mouth to speak; before I could say a word Mother was committed to not listening as she rose abruptly and left the room.

"Ok, so now what do we do" I rhetorically asked, "We talk to the doctor" and we left for the hospital.

We arrived at the hospital and immediately asked the front desk greeter to page Dr. Goodman. It seemed to take forever but in reality he responded within minutes. When the doctor appeared Jonathan and I approached him, first asking how Allison was and secondly how we could get her into a drug treatment facility.

"Let's go to my office – We'll have some privacy, and fresh coffee, there"

We entered his office and perched ourselves on his couch, directly in front of his desk. Too tense to sit back I sat on the edge of the couch, clutching my handbag in one hand and Jonathan's hand in the other.

"Coffee?" The doctor politely asked. I shook my head no; I knew I was too shaky to even consider holding a beverage. He poured himself some coffee then sat down behind his desk.

" Now, I see Allison had a good night - Her blood pressure is back to normal and her breathing is stabilized. I expect her to wake up at any time..." his voice trailed off as he continued looking at her chart

"She's never been to rehab?" he asked in a matter-of-fact manner.

"No, never... we didn't know, you know.. that she has a problem."

"You mean that she's an addict. You do know she has an addiction to Methamphetamine, correct?"

In a very small voice I responded "Yes."

"Good, now let's see what we can do to get her into rehab.... I'll have my staff check her insurance and then we'll see which facility is appropriate for her and her type of addiction, ideally she should go directly to treatment once she is discharged from the hospital - we don't want her to reconnect with people, places or things that could remind her of Methamphetamine or drugs in general. She'll be very vulnerable to abusing all drugs until she has had some treatment. Allison will have to agree to going to rehab and even better if she really and truly wants to stop using. Some people go but have no intention to stop using, they only want to appease family members. I hope that isn't the case with Allison but you never know. Is there anyone else we need to contact?

I hesitated, then piped up "Allison was living with our mother, we're going to need to tell her that Allison is going to rehab - I doubt this will make her happy... She doesn't understand, you know, the whole addiction thing, I barely understand it myself..." crying, I stopped talking. Dr.Goodman spoke up

"Allison is young and resilient, She's a perfect candidate for rehab and if she applies herself she's a perfect candidate for recovery. If you like, I can talk to your mother, after I talk to Allison. After all it's Allison's decision. We can't force her to go anywhere."

"I'd appreciate that"

"Good, I'll go speak to Allison now; you are both welcome to come along"

Nodding in agreement both Jonathan and I followed Dr. Goodman to Allison's room.

Allison's bed was raised up and she appeared to be awake when we entered her room. A slow sheepish grin crossed her face as she recognized us. Sitting next to her, I took her hand and she spoke first,

"Hey"

"Hey yourself lady" I replied. "I am so happy to see you" tears were streaming down both our faces as I leaned over and hugged her scrawny frame.

"Allison, this is Dr. Goodman, he's the doctor who admitted you"

Allison looked suspiciously at the doctor, not saying a word; she picked at an open sore on her face, causing droplets of blood to oozz to the surface of her skin. Realizing that she was still experiencing Meth delusions and behaviors Dr. Goodman took the opportunity to suggest inpatient rehab for Allison. Allison listened attentively and at first said nothing, just picked at her face. Then very softly she asked "What does Mom think?" Jonathan and I exchanged a quick glance, unsure of what to say. I feared telling Allison that Mother opposed rehab would be the excuse that Allison needed not to go for additional treatment.

"We are not sure your mother completely understands the complexity of addiction and the benefits of inpatient treatment" Dr. Goodman continued "Rehab would offer a safe, sober environment for you to adjust to not using any drugs or alcohol and give you some therapy to help you understand the reasons you turned to illegal drugs as well as what triggers you to use." Hesitating he added, "You don't need to decide right this second and regardless of your decision, I'd like you to stay hospitalized for one more night, just as a precaution"

"But I will need an answer by the end of the day so we can start a bed search and work with your insurance provider to get you into rehab as soon as possible, if that's what you decide."

"Ok, thank-you" Allison responded in the same soft tone, never making eye contact with the doctor.

"I'll be back later" and with a wink and nod Dr. Goodman was gone.

"So, what do you think?" I coyly asked Allison who appeared distant and aloft.

"I need to talk to Mother"

Fearing this would be her response, I tried to convince her that this was her decision and that Mother didn't really understand any of it.

"Mother always makes decisions for me – I need to talk to her, is she mad at me? Doesn't she want to see me? Maybe she doesn't love me anymore. What will I do without Mother?" Allison's apparent drug induced paranoia was in high gear as a nurse appeared with a sedative to calm Allison down.

"Now, now sugar, just relax and take a nap" the nurse's calming tones relaxed all of us as the sedative began to work almost instantly on Allison. Just as Allison's eyes began to close she whispered "Get Mom". And she was asleep.

Dr. Goodman had called Mother before we even arrived home to give her a ride to the hospital. Mother was ready and seemed eager to go as soon as we pulled up. Offering no conversation except that she had spoken to Allison's Dr., we rode in silence. When Allison woke, Me, Jonathan and Mother were by her side. Groggy and disoriented Allison asked for a glass of water, which all three of us scrambled to get for her. Mother sat next to Allison. Both appeared uncomfortable and not sure what to say. This was the first time Mother had seen Allison in almost two months and we were not sure if she was prepared for Allison's physical deterioration. Mother started her conversation as if she was at a ladies social – very polite, with light meaningless conversation. Mother completely ignored the sores on Allison's face, her gaunt frame and her Meth mouth. Mother talked about Allison's job and school and how those were the things that mattered. Mother chattered on that all Allison needed was to be busy. Mother attempted to jest about all the household chores they would have once they both were back home. Mother talked non-stop about everything BUT addiction, rehab and Methamphetamines.

The queen of denial had no intention of talking about the one subject that had brought us all to the hospital and to this point in our lives. For Allison, this was life or death and unbeknownst Mother was the grim reaper. Suddenly, without any warning, Allison spoke up. Her voice was strong and clear as she unmistakably stated "I'm going to rehab". Mother stopped talking, Jonathan's jaw dropped and I was just stunned as I stammered "Really? I'm sooo proud of you"

Before I could say another word Mother launched a verbal attack on all of us "Are you all crazy? Am I the only sane person left in this family? She is NOT a drug addict. She's just sowing her wild oats. She's had a tough childhood with no father ... Allison has learned her lesson and is fine now – Aren't you sweetie? You were just kidding us about rehab, weren't you? – You're coming home with me, to our home where things will go back to normal, just as they always were.... Allison matter-of-factly interrupted Mother

"I AM a drug addict and as far as being normal, I don't even know what that is. I've been hiding in the attic, from everyone and everything for what feels like forever. I don't have any real friends, just people I use with. I'm fearful of everyone and everything and I HATE MY LIFE. But if I could I'd get high right this minute without even thinking twice about it. I've never loved and hated anything as much as I do Meth. So if that is normal you can keep it, I'm ready to try something else. Tell Dr. Goodman I'm ready to sign the papers for rehab." Mother looked shocked and defeated. "If that's what you want Sweetie, of course you can go to rehab" Mother conceded, as she usually did when it came to Allison. This time I was grateful.

Authors post script

I welcome your stories, comments and questions

please write me at PO Box 12, Mt. Bethel, Pa 18343

Also, please be aware that
10% of net profits from this book will be donated to addiction
recovery organizations.

CPSIA information can be obtained at www.ICGtesting.com
Printed in the USA
LVOW13s0747030314

375738LV00001B/2/P